I0866636

THE POWER OF CONSCIOUS HUMAN PATTERNS

Colonel Sunil Prem is a retired Indian Army veteran, entrepreneur, innovator, trainer, speaker and author. He was the recipient of the President's Gold Medal in his army commissioning course. He served in the army for 23 years, before taking voluntary retirement. After retiring, he founded three successful companies in diverse fields. One of these companies, Brisk Olive Business Solutions Pvt. Ltd, has created a field force of veterans that is helping organizations grow across India, and providing training and employment opportunities to military veterans and spouses.

He is an electrical engineer. He topped in the BTech course he was pursuing at the College of Military Engineering, JNU, and obtained a perfect score of 10 in MTech at IIT Kanpur. He also has an MSc degree in Defence and Strategic Studies from Madras University.

He is married to Archana, a home baker, whom he credits with most of his successes in life. They have a son, a daughter and a dog. Col. Sunil Prem loves reading, writing and travelling in his free time.

THE POWER OF CONSCIOUS HUMAN PATTERNS

Achieve Success with ***Self-Mastery*** and ***Fulfilment***

SUNIL PREM

RUPA

Published by
Rupa Publications India Pvt. Ltd 2024
7/16, Ansari Road, Daryaganj
New Delhi 110002

Sales centres:
Bengaluru Chennai
Hyderabad Jaipur Kathmandu
Kolkata Mumbai Prayagraj

Illustration credit: Shreya Prem

P-ISBN: 978-93-6156-380-5
E-ISBN: 978-93-6156-504-5

First impression 2024

10 9 8 7 6 5 4 3 2 1

To my parents, who helped weave my patterns before
I even understood what they were.

Contents

Layer IV
The Core of the Onion: Success with Self-Mastery and Fulfilment

Appendices

Preface

Who Shapes Your Life?

'I don't like to gamble, but if there's one thing I'm willing to bet on, it's myself.'

—Beyoncé, American singer–songwriter

At the very outset, I would like to share a story, for this book is a story about the search for conscious human patterns.

What are human patterns? Well, they are the recurring rhythms—tiny and large—that we play out throughout our lives. They include our habits. But patterns are not our habits alone. Habits are what we do, while patterns include what we are. Habits are usually the effects of our patterns.

Patterns are the building blocks of our universe. They exist all around us. They also exist in our bodies, minds and emotions. They are present at every level of our being; in our genetic and involuntary systems; and at our unconscious, subconscious and conscious levels. They are present as rhythms in our activities, too—how our heart beats, how we breathe,

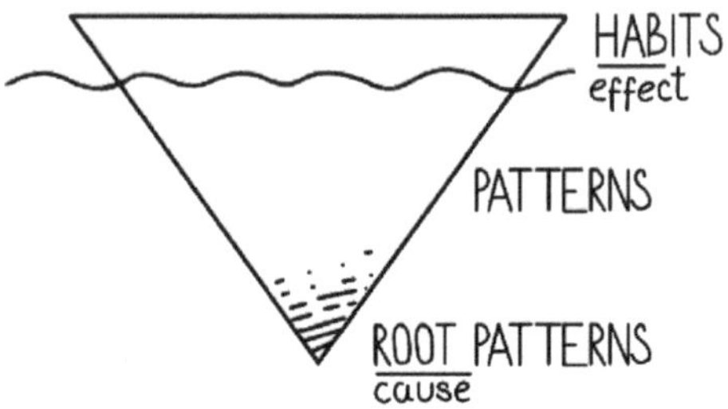

Fig. A: Habits are the visible parts of our patterns

sit, walk, talk, think and feel. All our complex activities, like professional responsibilities, finances and relationships, are mostly patterns.

Yet, a fish does not notice the water it lives in, even though it will not sustain if there is no water. Likewise, we scarcely, if ever, notice the patterns within and around us, even though they are responsible for almost everything in our lives.

I became aware of patterns very early on in life, by sheer chance. I discovered that consistently successful people thrive simply because of their consciously or unconsciously built patterns. Most of us overlook this fact because it is so incredibly simple. We do not notice the tiny patterns powering successful people. To us, such people appear superhuman and we start assuming that they are born with extraordinary abilities.

In this book, you will understand that you do not need to be born as a superhuman to succeed. You just need to be conscious of the patterns within and around you, and consciously shape them to get what you want.

Fig. B: Achieving your goals through patterns

There is something even more astounding.

By gaining conscious control over our patterns, we not only achieve success but also self-mastery and fulfilment in every moment and in every aspect of our life.

Don't we all want to feel successful and fulfilled?

It turns out that consciously mastering our patterns, achieving success and feeling fulfilled are part of the same virtuous cycle.

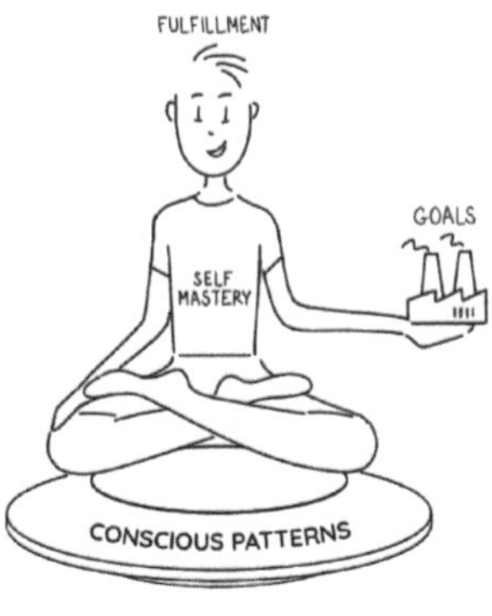

Fig. C: Success with self-mastery and fulfilment

The most astounding fact, however, is this: the right patterns are always easy and enjoyable. That is the beauty, simplicity and universality of the technique of conscious patterns. To be successful, your patterns should not be difficult for you.

The key to shaping patterns is consciousness. I have seen people reshape their bodies, alter their minds and rebuild their lives by consciously shaping their patterns. Conscious patterns are paths that take you where you want to go and make you what you want to be.

This has been my learning. So, the answer to the question 'who shapes your life?' is 'you!'

You know that already. But after reading this book, you will be able to achieve success with self-mastery and fulfilment, that too with ease. In fact, if it is not easy for you, then you know that you need to get your patterns right.

How to Read This Book

This book is 'exercises' interwoven into a story. To *be,* you must *do.*

The book starts with talking about what patterns are. It then moves on to the 'doing' part, where you learn how to reshape your own patterns.

The book is designed to be read in a sequence, from start to end. Each chapter leads to the next. The book is laid out in distinct parts (layers), so that you may choose what you wish to read, and in which sequence, to suit your self.

Spend a minute or two on each exercise. The 'starting' bit is the most important part of any journey. Thereafter, you can continue those exercises at your convenience.

Fig. D: Knowing and doing

The Book in a Nutshell

- Our environment is layers upon layers of interwoven patterns. The underlying patterns are always incredibly simple.
- Our bodies, minds, emotions and actions are structured in response to our patterned environment. Human intelligence and all our capabilities are merely the ability to recognize and respond to the patterns around us.
- These tiny patterns are so powerful that they define us. Yet, we are neither aware of most of them nor are we in control of them.
- You should become aware of your patterns in order to reshape and use them consciously. By doing so, you will become conscious beings in control of powerful patterns. The alternative is to be unconscious beings controlled by powerful, uncontrolled patterns.

- The right patterns make things easier and more organized. You should make a conscious attempt to look for ways in which almost anything that you want to do becomes enjoyable for you. If it is hard, then that pattern is not suited to you.
- By being aware and consciously shaping patterns—both internal and external—you can achieve success with self-mastery and fulfilment.

Thank you, dear reader, for joining me on this amazing journey.

As you start reading the book, I wish you success. Build your patterns, reach your goals, attain self-mastery and fulfilment, and enjoy the moments along your journeys, not just the destinations.

Introduction

Cracking the Code of Conscious Patterns

'We shall not cease from exploration, and the end of all our exploring will be to arrive where we started and know the place for the first time.'

—T.S. Eliot, poet

In 2010, I, a brand-new entrepreneur, was 46, broke and in the middle of a messy company break-up. It was perhaps the lowest point in my professional career.

After hitting rock bottom, I found two great companions. Humour, the first one, kept me laughing at my follies (and at a business partner, who was as badly off as me). The second one, introspection, took me to conscious patterns.

This is how the story unfolded.

In 2007, I had left the Indian Army after spending 27 glorious years since joining the National Defence Academy (NDA) as a 16-year-old. I did this because I wanted to spend more time with my family and try my hand at entrepreneurship. So, I started a company with a couple of friends. We planned to develop a software product for the security market. Parallel to that, I took up a job to support the company financially.

But as I said, that company bombed. Three years after we started, one of us walked out, claiming that the product was actually his. And as I had happily poured all my money into funding that product, I lost all of it.

This felt even more galling because I had been doing extremely well in the army. Very early on in life, I had become adept at using little actions—or tiny habits—to do things easily, and therefore effortlessly. Those little actions had unknowingly taken me to the top of my batch. I continued the same technique even after being commissioned as an officer. I would break things down into tiny bits and find ways to make them fun.

So, when I moved out of the army, I applied the same method. This time, however, it had failed. I was at a loss. I felt like a little boy whose favourite toy had suddenly stopped working. What was going on? What was I doing wrong?

I figured out one part of the answer easily. The armed forces work on complete trust among the comrades-in-arms. I had naively applied that same trust in the unknown, civilian world outside. I had known the army, but I did not know this new world. The result was obvious.

So, I became more cautious in dealing with the unknown. I did not, however, give up my underlying nature of expecting the best from others.

I wish I could say that, after this, I quickly figured out everything and emerged victorious, but that did not happen.

Yes, I got up, dusted myself off, started again and co-founded another company. Here, I again applied whatever I had learnt so far. This time, the company succeeded (and continues to do well). But this was not the effortless success that I had been used to; there were too many confusions and grey areas.

My new company developed custom software for business clients, but I knew nothing about software. To me, at the time, http and html looked the same (software folks will get the joke). Object-oriented programming (OOP), the prevailing programming paradigm, too seemed incomprehensible because 'how could software model things?' At the time, I was only aware of functional programming, which is a lot like algebra. I also knew nothing of the corporate world, the various industries, sales, marketing, finances, networking, and so on.

I again used tiny routines to make my work easier. I also tried to learn everything that I could about my new world. Soon, I learnt enough about software, business, etc., to get by, and the company began to do reasonably well. But it took intense effort.

Haven't you experienced that feeling when an answer is somewhere in your mind but scattered like the pieces of a puzzle that do not fit together—all because one key piece is missing? I was overlooking something very simple.

So, I searched all over. That search lasted eight years. It was not a leave-all-else-aside kind of search. But at the back of my mind, I was always seeking the answer.

During that time, I read, watched and tried to understand works of renowned people in their respective fields. I learnt a lot. Some of that knowledge overlapped my own findings. But I could not get rid of the feeling that something was missing there, too. For example, everyone referred to the same basic principles for success in life and advised people to develop certain key skills and attitudes, or habits, to succeed. But if these skills and habits were so critical, then why were they not easy? Why did it take so much of effort to develop them? Why would they work for some people and not for others? Why would they work in one context but not in another? Nature could not be so stupid as to have deliberately made all good things tough to master. There had to be a rational answer. Yet, I could not find it.

So, I began to experiment on my own. That's what the army had taught us: 'When in doubt, return to the basics.'

I can't list the hundreds of things that I tried. But many of those random experiments led to seemingly strange findings. For example, I was amazed to find that whenever I did a headstand in the morning, I would lose my temper later in the day, no matter how hard I tried not to be irritable. Similarly, if I placed a weight, like even my hand, over my heart, and fell asleep, a nightmare would almost surely follow. I also noticed that if I combined an absorbing conscious activity 'A' (like holding an extremely important conversation on the phone) with a conscious or subconscious activity 'B' (like climbing stairs), then activity B climbing those stairs turned into 'zero conscious effort'. This was even if activity B seemed like an effort when done in the absence of activity A. I would climb from the basement to the twenty-sixth floor, where I stayed, all the while staying on an extremely absorbing phone call, often without feeling even an iota of effort. Climbing the stairs would become a subconscious activity for me. And so on and so forth, I experimented with and analysed such activities and outcomes.

Apparently, my irritation after a headstand had something to do with the excess blood pumped into the head due to being upside down. Soon, I found the solution. By getting into the legs-over-your-shoulders pose (plough pose) and the dead-man pose (*shavasana*) immediately following a headstand, the irritation I was experiencing disappeared. These postures apparently redistributed blood back into my entire body. I found similar simple explanations for other outcomes, too.

The ability to switch on and switch off pain, anger and effort at will was a life-altering discovery for me. I repeatedly practised this ability by consciously using bodily, mental and environmental triggers. It worked each time. Conclusions began to bubble up in my mind.

It seemed that feelings, emotions, thoughts and actions could be voluntarily created, eliminated or altered by finding the underlying causes and what one has to do (or be) to bring about the desired outcomes. And these outcomes and actions would themselves become causes, looping back to one's body, thoughts, emotions and actions. This created a virtuous cycle.

Most importantly, I found that this logic worked for everything including body, mind, emotions, energy and actions. All of these turned out to be controllable to a large extent.

But if that is considered true, won't one's body, mind, emotions and energy be merely tools? And what of the world outside of oneself? How does one deal with that—that, surely, is not completely controllable.

Suddenly, all the pieces of the puzzle that I had been trying to decipher for a lifetime fell into place.

I realized my fundamental error of omission. Despite having eyes, I was not looking at the obvious. All my life, I had considered humans special and, therefore, complex. I had also considered the world around, things like OOP, marketing, sales, success, etc., somehow complex and, therefore, magical. The realization dawned on me that everything—humans included—was simple and bound by the same laws.

Many years ago, I met someone who quoted something like this to me, '*Utho, jao, aur woh paa lo jo tumne kabhi khoya hi nahin tha* (Get up, go and find that what you had never lost).' It took me a while, but I finally understood what he had meant.

I had searched everywhere and found that the solution already lay with me. The causes for my successes and failures were the tiny patterns within and around me. The patterns within me were not just my habits. These were all the genetic, involuntary, unconscious, subconscious and conscious patterns and rhythms within me. These existed in my bodily geometry, mind, emotions and actions. My habits were the results of these underlying patterns. Knowing these underlying patterns and controlling them consciously was the key to success.

Of course, not everything about me could be changed. I could not, for example, change my height or my genes. Similarly, I could not understand or change all the patterns around me.

That is where our consciousness becomes important. Our consciousness helps us understand and deal with what we do not know. What we already know, we turn into patterns.

I could now see that all that seemed abstract, complex and confusing within and outside me was actually simple underneath. I only needed to find and work upon the simple patterns underlying my complex-looking world.

It was from this moment onwards that I consciously began to search for the simple underlying causes within and outside of myself. I already knew how to redesign things to make them fun for myself. I combined the two learnings.

Almost instantly, things began to change. For years, I had suffered from brain fog and fatigue around noon. It was so debilitating at times that I would often curl up for an hour or so to recover. But the moment I understood that the root causes of this had to be logical and, therefore, simple, I began to notice them. The key reason for the brain fog turned out to be simply not blinking enough! I had never noted earlier that I rarely blinked while working continuously on my laptop for hours on end. To eliminate this underlying cause—not blinking enough—I found an exercise. It involved tossing a ball from one hand to another and blinking after catching the ball. It was a good exercise but very boring. So, I redesigned it. I learnt to juggle, and began juggling between work breaks, blinking after I caught each ball. Now, my afternoon brain fog and fatigue are things of the past. I have also turned into an amateur juggler!

In addition, there was a new business that I wanted to start. It was modelled around rehabilitating ex-soldiers and using their skills to transform society. This time, instead of focussing on seemingly complex business outcomes, I consciously worked on the tiny underlying patterns that comprise various business processes. I also made the patterns fun for myself and my employees. This new company has grown considerably in a very short time. Though it was not my intention to start the company, it might even turn into a unicorn in some time.

In the years that followed my eureka moment, I have also attained financial freedom, which was something that had eluded me earlier due to certain ignored underlying patterns. I was also able to find time for my family and friends; I was able to travel, write two books apart from this one; and I continue to do all that I have wanted to in life.

However, I do not claim to have found something hitherto undiscovered. I have found that, throughout history, philosophers and scientists have both observed and described the underlying order and symmetry in our world. They have conveyed this to us through stoicism, yoga and zen; the words of Marcus Aurelius and Krishna; social and religious texts, like the Bhagavad Gita and the Bible; or through societal norms, rituals and scientific laws. They have noted the presence and immense power of simple patterns and rules, and the role of our consciousness in shaping those and us.

All that I have done is stand on the shoulders of these giants to decipher and convey the power of those patterns and consciousness, unified into a simple philosophy suited to my own times.

I have found patterns and consciousness to be an inseparable continuum. And I have found that, through consciousness and the application of patterns, you can achieve self-mastery and a sense of fulfilment, along with success.

What exactly did I discover? How could you use it? In Chapter 1, I attempt to summarize everything.

PATTERNS

1

An Overview of Conscious Patterns

'You can't connect the dots looking forward;
you can only connect them looking backwards.'

—Steve Jobs, former CEO of Apple

Our World is Made of Patterns

Our entropical universe, which seems complex and disorderly, is built up of layers and layers of simple patterns. Look around and you will find repeating rhythms and patterns everywhere. Almost everything around, down to the subatomic particle, is built following some blueprint or the other that repeats itself.

The creation of these rhythms and patterns is not an accident. During evolution, patterns are the most favoured forms of energy propagation. This makes patterns the building blocks of nature.

We humans turn into excellent recognizers and creators of patterns in response to the patterns around us. Our breathing, heartbeats, thoughts, feelings, the way we sit, walk, talk, our circadian and ultradian rhythms, the way we work, maintain our relationships, manage finances, and even the most complex activities we perform mostly turn into patterns. We become patterned at every level—genetic, involuntary, unconscious, subconscious and conscious.

These Patterns are Simple, Yet Immensely Powerful

Superficially, many of the patterns—inside and outside of us—appear complex and uncontrollable.

But the most complex- and abstract-looking things have simple rhythms and patterns underlying them. Our habits that look complex and uncontrollable, too, have simple roots or causes underlying them.

However, our popular culture has focussed more on our superficial habits, missing out on the simple causes. Most advice given on habits is generic. Habits themselves are defined in generic and immeasurable terms, like procrastination, fear and reliability. Advice on changing habits often does not tell us why these immeasurable abstractions (habits) exist and exactly what (in measurable terms) should we do to alter them.

Consider this analogy. Your car breaks down and you go to a car mechanic, who says, 'Sorry, sir. Your car does not feel like working today,' or, 'That's just how your car is built,' or he tells the car, 'Come on, baby! Don't be lazy. Don't procrastinate. Start working!'

A car, however, is neither built to be lazy nor procrastinate. It is a simple machine. There have to be simple reasons underlying any defect. One needs to identify and correct those reasons or root causes for the car to start working again.

But while working on ourselves, we assume, crazily, that we are complex—unlike a car—and that no simple root cause exists in our case. Therefore, we focus on abstract concepts, like laziness, incompetence or complex inabilities at work, business and relationships. We focus on creating the effects we want, like will power, perseverance and confidence, by focussing on changing the effects themselves. That is like trying to cure a disease by only controlling the fever. Such approaches rarely work, or are much tougher to accomplish even if they do.

We, however, do not focus on the underlying causes, which could be anything—they are usually simple, measurable and, therefore, controllable. And those causes could be both within and around us. Those underlying patterns or causes can be immensely powerful because patterns are repetitive.

Nothing can match the power of your ceaseless rhythms and patterns. As per my findings, 22,000 uneven breaths a day can kill your energy, while a mere clear nose and chest, along with rhythmic breathing, can boost your energy and physical power, kill infections and allergies, improve your quality of sleep, sharpen your mind, and harmonize emotions to lead you to better relationships and success in professional and personal life. It is known that 10,000 steps each day, wearing worn out or badly designed footwear, can destroy your knees, whereas just wearing the right footwear can make your knees less prone to complications.

The tiny aligned rhythms of your body, mind, emotions, energy, actions and environment power you on, moment to moment, to outcomes that cannot be achieved through random surges of effort or by fluke. No 30-minute exercise routine can overcome the effects of millions of moments of a sedentary lifestyle. No back exercise will relieve the incessant impact of a bad posture. No single brilliant insight can overcome the results of a continually wayward mind. No limited period of coherence can overcome the effects of your continually chaotic environment.

In effect, the right little patterns are the ones that power you towards an amazing life.

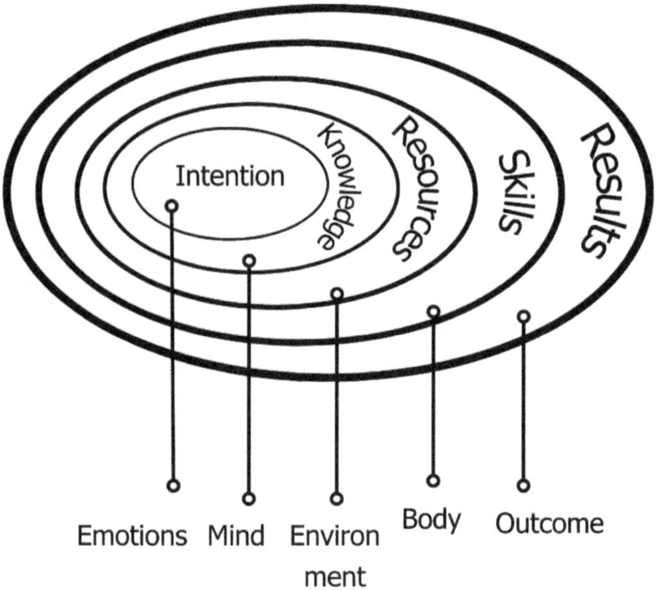

Fig. 1.1: The patterns of your environment, emotions, mind, body and outcomes define what you are and what you can achieve

Paradoxically, while most of our patterns are beautifully fashioned by nature to support us, there are also those that block us and lead us to failures and discomfort. Fortunately, nature has designed us such that they can be changed.

The Key to Controlling Our Patterns is Our Conscious Awareness

Nature is smart. To control our patterns, it has given us conscious awareness.

For example, our minds are imprinted with our past experiences and emotions because those are critical to our survival. But some of these past experiences might no longer be useful to us today. They could even subvert our current lives.

Nature has, therefore, also given us the tool to remove such causes that do not support us any longer. That tool is our conscious awareness; it is the key to control our patterns. That is how the phrase 'conscious patterns' came to be coined.

Fig 1.2: Conscious patterns

Conscious awareness is the 'meta' state of being outside of oneself. It means observing one's own self and one's surrounding as a detached observer. It allows a person to analyse situations objectively. In such a state, the mind is both cognizant of and responsive to surroundings, while observing and rationally accepting underlying truths. Such awareness leads us to the objective reality of our patterns. By being aware of the patterns within and around, you can turn them into conscious patterns.

With this awareness and understanding, everything changes. We start focussing on the right things. By becoming aware of the tiny patterns that comprise most of us and our world, we obtain the keys to changing ourself.

There is another way of looking at this. The ultimate purpose of patterns is to support our conscious existence.

We are conscious beings. Our bodies, minds, emotions and actions are built to deal with both the expected and the unexpected. Our patterns help us deal with the expected and the routine. They free our analytical minds from the burden of the expected and the routine, of what has been, of what we already know and have resolved for ourselves. By using patterns, we free our minds to deal with the unexpected and the unpredictable. Consciously, we can explore, imagine and create new things.

Conscious beings, without patterns, would perhaps be theorists. Maybe they would be able to imagine new realities and possibilities, but without the means to create those realities. All their energy would be exhausted in dealing with chaos. With patterns working genetically, involuntarily, unconsciously, subconsciously and consciously in our environment, we become creators.

On the other hand, patterned beings, without conscious awareness, would be like animals. They would not exercise choices or create anything new. They would just follow patterns blindly. That is not what nature fashioned us humans to be.

Consciousness and patterns are, therefore, inseparable. Each exists because of the other and for the other. Hence, our goal is to understand not patterns alone but conscious patterns.

Shaping Patterns Is Easy Once We Figure Out What to Focus On

It was easy for me to excel in the army. Everything that we had to do there was mostly spelled out for us. Even the processes that were to be followed were mostly already worked out to perfection. The only problem left was to find out how to do those things while also having fun. And since I had already cracked that problem—by creating tiny repetitive rhythms that suited me—I was able to succeed.

But once outside, in the big wide world with many rules, I realized that one also needed to understand the factors influencing our outcomes. My financial problems, including the ones related to the business, were the results of not understanding their simple underlying causes. This led to misalignments between the results I wanted and my patterns (rhythms of skills, actions, emotions, beliefs and thoughts).

Shaping patterns is easy if we focus on the roots instead of the shoots. This is because the roots are fewer and each root leads to a thousand shoots.

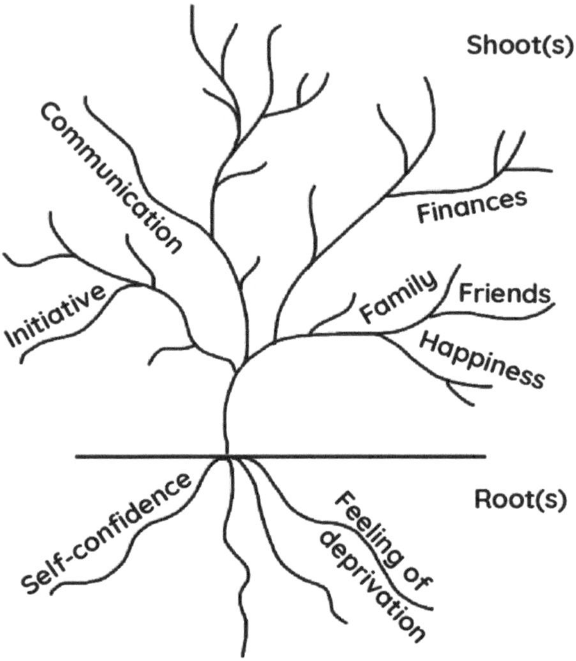

Fig. 1.3: A few roots lead to thousands of shoots

Changing these root patterns is not just easy, you can also make the process fun for yourself. In fact, the right patterns should be easy and enjoyable for you.

Changes in our root patterns are not temporary, the way changes in our habits often are. When we work on our superficial habits, they sometimes disappear, only to reappear soon. This is because habits are merely reflections of underlying patterns through countless mirrors. We try to change our habits, but we only end up subduing or hiding them by covering those mirrors with the drapes of our superficial actions. But the moment those drapes slip, the root patterns reassert themselves with a vengeance and our old habits reappear. That is why working on superficial habits alone often fails or requires immense hard work.

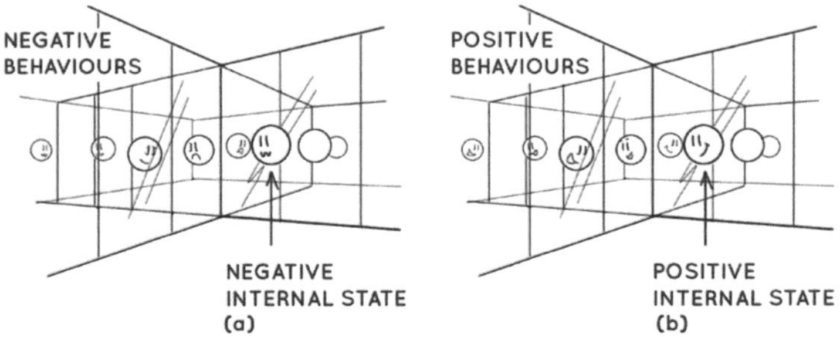

Fig. 1.4: Your behaviour is the reflection of your internal state

For example, imagine a person who is perpetually lethargic. Also, assume that the root cause of their lethargy is dehydration. Now such people might attend courses and read self-help books and force themselves to become energetic. They might even succeed for a while. But will they be able to sustain the change? Ultimately they will collapse or fall sick or revert to their earlier state because the root cause still lies unaddressed.

Often in life, people also combine two wrong methods while trying to reach the right outcome. This happens because they mindlessly adopt a path or an apparent shortcut instead of consciously looking for the right path.

Here is an example. A particular employee in my company usually did not coordinate with her other colleagues and rarely provided feedback. To overcome this, her manager would start each day with an all-hands coordination meeting. That took up an hour of all the 20-odd persons in that department.

They achieved the desired result but at what cost? Now, there were two wrong patterns in the scenario: (a) the one employee still not coordinating or learning how to, and (b) a needless meeting each morning that wasted everyone's time.

This is like travelling 20 km one way, and returning 19 km another way, only to get to the destination which was just 1 km away from the starting point!

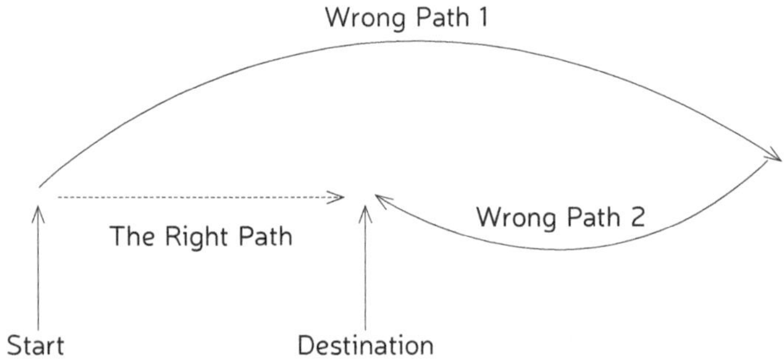

Fig. 1.5: Wrong paths might take you to your destination, but the journey will be very hard

Now imagine this happening on a grand scale. Imagine a scenario where you try to reach an outcome, but while compensating for errors you end up adding more errors, without ever having sorted out the root cause that led to the error in the first place. Is it a wonder then that the right outcomes in life appear to be so hard to reach?

Also, reshaping root patterns consciously in an attempt to restructure your life will be like reshaping a forest without pruning some of the trees. Instead, you should plant new seeds. As the new seeds take root, the entire forest will be transformed eventually.

Fig. 1.6: Changing the forest by seeding 'new patterns'

Patterns Lead to Success with Self-Mastery and Fulfilment

The consciously shaped patterns in our bodies, minds, emotions, energies and environment also make us feel fulfilled in our current moments. We humans are simply energy underneath. This energy distinguishes life from all lifeless things; it expresses itself by causing change. We label these changes as success, power, achievement, etc.

Our energy must express itself completely, effectively and in the right direction. It must not remain trapped, be ineffectual or misdirected, or cause us unease.

Mastering our ceaseless patterns causes us to express ourselves completely and effectively at each moment. It leads to accomplishment and a sense of inner peace in each moment. That feeling is what we call fulfilment.

Success without such personal growth or self-mastery, on the other hand, does not lead us to fulfilment. This is why those who seem to have everything in the eyes of others, still work to achieve that sense of fulfilment and growth. This is also why those who succeed by fluke, without personal growth and self-mastery, feel like failures from within.

The book *Ikigai: The Japanese Secret to a Long and Happy Life,* by Hector Garcia and Francesc Miralles, uses the word 'flow' to describe the state of fulfilment. It is in this state that we stop caring about the passage of time, and just flow in complete harmony with the present moment.

When correctly applied, conscious patterns also lead to all-round success in every aspect of life. And isn't that what we all seek? That is the beauty of tiny, conscious patterns.

The Technique of Creating Patterns Is Simple

It includes finding:

- The right patterns in and around us, which are causes, not effects.
- The right methods that will reshape those patterns.
- The right methods that suit us, and are, therefore, easy and fun for us (or we find ways of making such methods fun—this is much easier than you think).
- The right techniques for executing these methods.

Back to the Beginning

I have now laid out what you must do. In order to make the right methods an enjoyable experience for yourself, you must discover the concept of developing conscious patterns sequentially, like peeling the layers of an onion, one layer at a time, and gaining complete understanding of it till you are ready for the next layer. In doing so, you will reach the core easily and achieve success along with self-mastery and fulfilment.

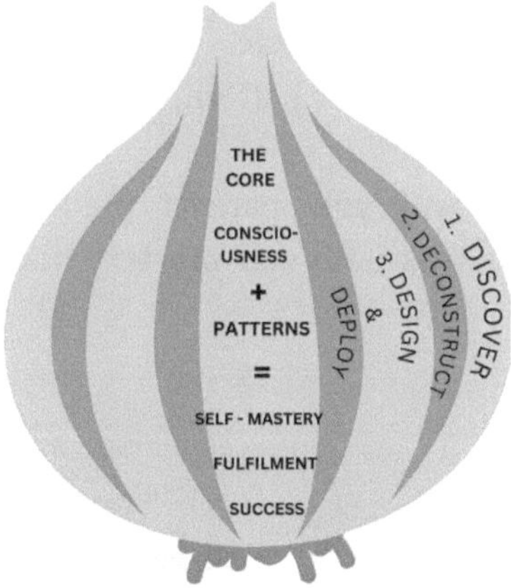

Fig. 1.7: The onion of conscious patterns

This book is similarly laid out in layers (or parts):

- **Layer 1: Discover patterns**
- **Layer 2: Deconstruct patterns**
- **Layer 3: Design and deploy your own patterns**
  - To design your own patterns, use the repeating rhythm of PACE, which stands for:
    - **Picture** or **plan** your outcomes.
    - Become **aware** of the patterns that lead to those outcomes.
    - **Craft** or **create** those patterns within and around you.

    - **Evolve** those patterns.
  - Crafting each pattern is a further simple four-step sub-process called **BERT**:
    - **Blueprint** a pattern by using the methods and techniques that are right for you.
    - **Enable** your pattern by modifying your environment and yourself, using a variety of techniques like cues, rewards, anchors, etc.
    - **Rhythmize** your pattern by setting up rhythms and routines.
    - **Tinker** with your pattern to eliminate any kink.
- **The core: Success with self-mastery and fulfilment**

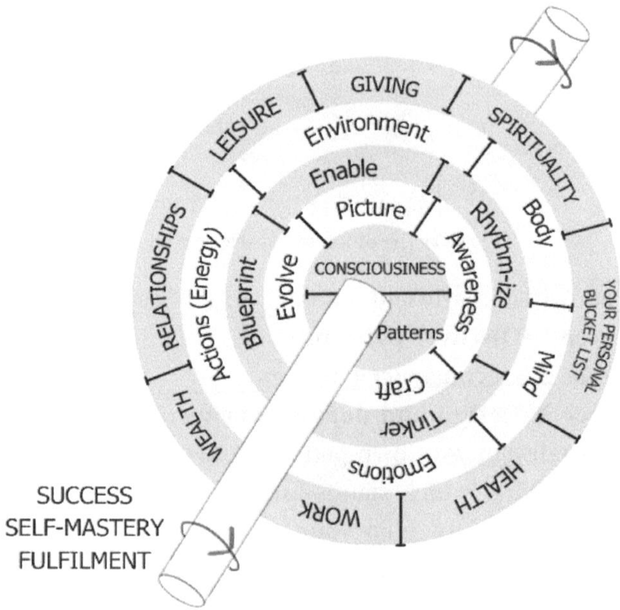

Fig. 1.8: The flywheel of conscious patterns

The first step itself, 'Discovering Patterns', will take you ahead by leaps and bounds. For example, for sorting out my finances, all I needed was the realization that I was stuck in the pattern of not caring about my finances. Once I realized this, it was hardly a problem. I simply entrusted my friend and brilliant wealth consultant, Vijay Pruthi, with managing my finances. Another example is that of a friend who took a long time to realize that his habit of constant unhealthy snacking was the key reason behind his weight gain. Once he understood this in measurable terms, he simply changed his habit and his excess weight disappeared.

The second step, 'Deconstructing Patterns', too helps in eliminating many unwanted patterns and reinforcing better ones. An ex-soldier friend, the youngest of four brothers, was stuck with the belief 'you [I] can't do it'. This had been branded into his unconscious mind by his older brothers when he was a kid. The moment he came to identify and realize that it was his limiting root emotion, his problem became more or less sorted.

As you begin to 'Design and Deploy Your Patterns' to work for you in an aligned manner, they become your inexorable force-multipliers.

So, let us continue this wonderful journey that will help you craft your conscious patterns and create the results you want.

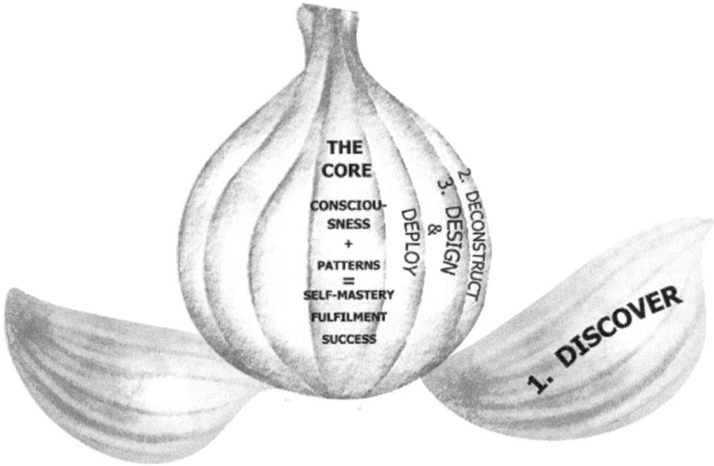

Layer I: Discover Patterns

'There are only patterns, patterns on top of patterns, patterns that affect other patterns. Patterns hidden by patterns. Patterns within patterns…

'What we call chaos is just patterns we haven't recognized. What we call random is just patterns we can't decipher. What we can't understand we call nonsense. What we can't read we call gibberish.'

—Chuck Palahniuk, *Survivor*

2

What Are Patterns?

'YOUTH: You do believe that the world is, in all ways, a simple place?

PHILOSOPHER: Yes, this world is astonishingly simple and life itself is, too.'

—Ichiro Kishimi and Fumitake Koga, *The Courage to be Disliked*

Simply put, a pattern is a design, arrangement or sequence that follows a regular, consistent or repetitive order. It can also be called a model or a blueprint made for replication.

A set of lines is a pattern, and so are waves in water; they follow a rhythm, a recurring pattern.

Once we become aware of patterns and rhythms, we begin to see them everywhere. All our senses begin to notice patterns.

Patterns as Fundamental Units of Nature

Patterns in nature can take many forms. They can resemble the branches and leaves of a tree, tornadoes, the seeds in a sunflower, a meandering stream, the explosion of a supernova or a volcano, or the closely packed units in a beehive.

It does not matter how we classify patterns. What matters is that nature is fundamentally patterned and filled with symmetry.

In an article in 1972, Nobel laureate Philip W. Anderson wrote, 'It is only slightly overstating the case to say that physics is the study of symmetry.'[1]

Keith J. Devlin, accomplished mathematician, educator and professor at Stanford University, says in his book, *Mathematics: The Science of Patterns,* that mathematics is nothing but the study of possible patterns that exist around us, real or imagined, visual or mental, arising from the natural world or from within the human mind. In another book, he writes, 'Abstract patterns are the very essence of thought, of communication, of computation, of society, and of life itself.'[2]

Director of Engineering at Google, futurist and entrepreneur, Ray Kurzweil, in his book *How to Create a Mind: The Secret of Human Thought Revealed*, argues that pattern recognition and intelligence are essentially the same thing.

Seen this way, mathematics, physics, chemistry, biology, psychology, engineering, design, the rest of the sciences

---

[1]Martin, Joseph D., 'Prestige Asymmetry in American Physics: Aspirations, Applications, and the Purloined Letter Effect', *Science in Context*, Vol. 30, No. 4, 2017, pp. 475–506.

[2]Devlin, Keith J., *Sets, Functions, And Logic: An Introduction to Abstract Mathematics,* CRC Press LLC, US, 2003.

and arts, recipes, melodies, sports, theorems, laws and all human pursuits are the conscious recognition, creation and application of some fundamental patterns. We seek patterns to resolve things we find complex.

This takes us to a powerful conclusion: It is not coincidence that we humans are made up of patterns. We are but an extension of the patterned world around us. It took me years to figure out this incredibly obvious fact.

Humans as Bundles of Patterns

You'll be amazed to find the extent and the depth to which patterns exist within us.

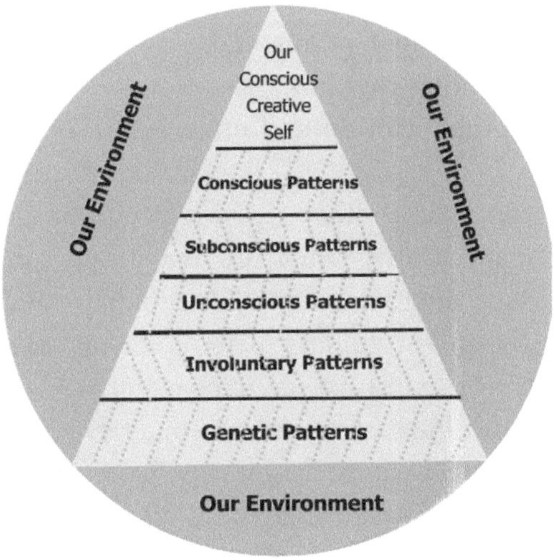

Fig. 2.1: Levels at which our human bodies, minds, emotions and actions are patterned through interactions with our environment: genetic, involuntary, unconscious, subconscious and conscious. These patterns enable our conscious creative self.

1. **Genetic Level:** A person's genes—those basic physical and functional units of heredity—are unique. But even at the genetic level, we find the same A, T, C and G nucleotide bases arranged in different patterns. (Now that you know this detail, simply forget it. Just understand that patterns extend to our genes, too. They transmit learnings from one generation to another.)
2. **(So-called) Involuntary Level:** These are parts of us that we cannot (or at least we think we cannot) totally or partially control:
    - Our involuntary body is deeply patterned. If you look at your heartbeat monitor, you will see an involuntary pattern there. Our digestive system, nervous system, lymphatic system, etc., also follow patterns. Our cells grow, fight germs and regenerate themselves in never-ending rhythms.
    - Our minds drift on and off as we wake up and go to sleep.
    - Our anger and other repetitive emotions, like hunger and pain, mostly bubble up and subside on their own.
    - We take approximately 22,000 breaths a day. That is mostly an involuntary pattern. Sweat, salivation and sneezing are also involuntary patterns.

    These involuntary patterns matter. Suppose you procrastinate because you never have the energy and, therefore, always fail. Imagine if all of this is happening only because of your inability to breathe right. Wouldn't working on your breathing change your results by some percentage?

    Can we alter these involuntary patterns?

John Clarke, MD, writes in the book *Science of Breath*: 'Biofeedback research has shown that some of the physiological activities of these (our) organs previously labelled involuntary, can be consciously controlled with training, although much practice is usually required to become proficient in consciously controlling these organs.'[3]

In 1970, in an American research laboratory, Swami Rama, an Indian yogi, demonstrated how he could stop his heart at will. Linda Johnson describes this experiment in the foreword to the book *Science of Breath*: 'Under the most rigorous experimental conditions, he simulated death by virtually stopping his brain waves and heartbeat, and yet remained fully conscious of events occurring around him in the laboratory.'[4]

It seems we can control our involuntary selves through suitable means.[5] This allows us to control our metabolism, bodily functions, emotional states, thoughts and whatnot. The effects are countless and impact every outcome of ours!

3. **Unconscious Level:** Above this involuntary level we have patterns at the level of what psychologist Carl Jung called the unconscious mind.
   - Our bodies react unconsciously to most stimuli in a patterned manner. One example can be how most of

[3]Rama, Swami, Rudolph Ballentine and Alan Hymes, *Science of Breath*, Himalayan Institute Press, Honesdale, USA, 1998.

[4]Ibid.

[5]Our breathing, a unique function that is both voluntary and involuntary, can be used to control at least some of our internal systems. Pranayama, the yogic science of breathing, works on this premise. Read more about breathing exercises in *Science of Breath*.

us unconsciously shape ourselves to be like our closest friends.

- The same applies to our minds. We generate around 12,000–60,000 thoughts each day but with little conscious control over them. Don't most of our thoughts follow set patterns?[6] Are we not repeatedly being subjective or objective, positive or negative, attentive or inattentive? Imagine someone saying, 'Hi, how are you?' One person responds by thinking, 'She likes me!' and another thinks, 'Ooh! So, she found the time to wish me today! I wonder what she wants from me.' So, two people observe the same event but interpret it totally differently. Both are also mostly unconscious to the reason as to why they respond the way they do.
- We always experience certain emotions in certain situations. It often happens that as soon as we think about something, we immediately frown or smile, unconscious of our reaction unless someone points it out. We are unconscious of many of our actions from moment to moment.

4. **Subconscious Level:** Fourthly, there is the subconscious level at which we are only dimly or peripherally aware of what is happening. A common example is driving. Don't we sometimes reach some place but cannot recall how we got there? Similarly, we follow our own unique

[6]I have tested this repeatedly with varied subjects. A person, for example, on hearing about another person, always comes up with the same remark, with nearly the same words. It is as if there is a hard-wired connection in the brain that leads to those words whenever the person encounters an associated event.

subconscious patterns of walking, talking, eating, drinking, smiling, laughing, working, etc.

Combined together, the above four levels probably constitute at least 95 per cent of our lives.[7] There is an enormous amount of ongoing research on what consciousness awareness means and what lies beyond it. But my guess is that the patterns that exist beyond our consciousness awareness far exceed even 95 per cent of our lives and what we are. And if this figure is proven to be correct, it implies that at least 95 per cent of who we are or what we do is not conscious.

5. **Conscious Level:** Then, there is also the conscious part of our beings that consciously thinks, decides, feels and acts. This part of our lives, too, is mostly patterns. In a patterned manner, we wake up and have a cup of coffee, brush, bathe, read, write, work, watch TV, engage in our hobbies, make decisions, and so on.

   These symmetries extend even to large and seemingly complex activities, like how we make plans, do our jobs, run our businesses, manage our finances, and behave in our relationships. All the songs and symphonies that we hear and compose, the stories we narrate, the books we read and write, the sports we participate in and practise are recurring versions of some fundamental blueprints.

   If we scratch the surface of our most complex-seeming conscious activities or break them into micro-segments, we will find the same repetitive patterns there

---

[7]Goleman, Daniel, 'New View of Mind Gives Unconscious an Expanded Role', *The New York Times*, 7 February 1984, https://tinyurl.com/29m3mj3v. Accessed on 10 April 2024.

too, with our responses to triggers remaining almost exactly the same.

For years, I have observed my mother react to the mention of a particular aunt with exactly the same words, 'Oh, she's had it so good in life!' Her neural pathways have possibly hard-wired that thought.

Understanding Environment

Our environment is deeply patterned. Right from the sun rising each morning, to the climate we live in, the people and things we associate with, or do not, everything is mostly patterned. Further, how we use and manage our time is also patterned. Everything exists within time and space. Time is our ultimate resource. Without time, life and existence are meaningless.

We divide our time into:

- **Our Present:** Our present is what exists now. We have already seen how deeply patterned that is.
- **Our Past:** Our present and future are guided by our past. Therefore, we carry it with us at all levels—as patterns in our genes and involuntary systems, in our unconscious, subconscious and conscious awareness.
- **Our Future:** Our future is an imagined reality that is equally necessary. Without a future to guide us, we cannot even take the next step. We carry our future with us in our bodies, minds, emotions and actions. Every atom and every cell in our body knows what to do next. Our imagination of our future, too, is patterned.

Add all these patterns and maybe 99 per cent of what we are or do is patterns. All of this happens throughout our lives, mostly without us even noticing it. We, at the most, usually notice only our habits, the top of the inverted icebergs of patterns. And together, all these patterns come to define who we are, what we can or cannot do, and what becomes of us.

But where do these patterns come from? That is the next question we must answer.

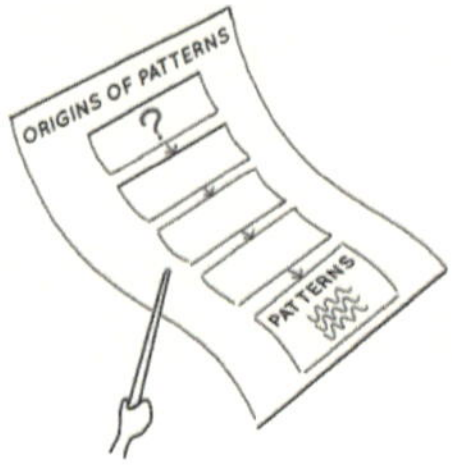

3

The Origins of Patterns

'When solving problems, dig at the roots instead of just hacking at the leaves.'

—Anthony J. D'Angelo,
author, speaker and business owner

In the 1930s and 1940s, a renowned Canadian neurosurgeon, Dr Wilder Penfield, made some amazing discoveries while conducting brain surgeries. He published these findings in his books and papers.[8] Thomas A. Harris, MD, a prominent American psychiatrist and psychoanalyst, made these discoveries widely known through his landmark book *I'm OK – You're OK.*[9]

This is what Penfield found in his experiments:

- During our early lives, our brain acts like a recorder. It records, in detail, everything that is in our awareness—

[8]'Wilder Penfield Publications', *Neurotree,* https://tinyurl.com/3azhwkc4. Accessed on 10 April 2024.

[9]Harris, T. A., *I'm OK - You're OK*, Arrow Books, 1995.

the words of a song, the details of an event, or the smell of the earth on a rainy day. By using a weak electric current to stimulate their temporal cortex, which is located at the front of the brain, Penfield was able to make patients replay or recall their 'recordings'.[10]

- Now comes the astounding part. Penfield also found that our brain doesn't just record what we see, hear, smell, etc. It also records what we feel during those events. Those associated feelings are inextricably linked with the memories of those events stored in our minds. So, if we heard a song in the past while we were happy, that feeling of happiness gets imprinted and linked with our memory of that song. Similarly, if we felt scared when we were scolded by our parents, that feeling of fear, too, gets stored and in the future, we might end up feeling scared every time someone we consider to be an authority figure, like our parent, gets angry with us.
- In our day-to-day experiences, certain events cause us to replay these past recordings. For example, when an authority figure shouts at us, we replay our recording of our angry father or mother, along with our original feelings. This recall is like actually reliving that event, as if it were happening to us now, all over again.
- The sequence followed in these involuntary recollections is: (1) reliving (spontaneous, involuntary feeling) and (2) remembering (conscious voluntary thinking about

[10]Penfield, Wilder, and Edwin Boldrey, 'Somatic Motor and Sensory Representation in the Cerebral Cortex of Man as Studied by Electrical Stimulation', *Brain*, Vol. 60, No. 4, 1937, pp. 389–443, tinyurl.com/572fr658. Accessed on 20 May 2024.

that past event). Penfield reported that the reliving part can happen without remembering. What he meant was that we might hear a melody and feel happy, but we might not be able to recall why. Similarly, we might feel scared whenever a boss acts aggressively, even though we might not recall what causes us to feel that way.

- Penfield reported the case of a woman who would feel an overwhelming sense of melancholy on hearing a particular song. Later, she recalled her mother playing that song on the piano around the time she died. After her mother's death, the woman, who was a child of five at the time, became severely depressed. Years later, those feelings surfaced in the woman when she heard the same song, even though she could not initially recall the link.[11]
- Penfield found that the human mind utilizes its past recordings to interpret its current experiences. To quote, 'These recorded experiences and feelings associated with them are available for replay today in as vivid a form as when they happened and provide much of the data which determines the nature of today's interactions.'[12]

Penfield also talked of patterns in his conclusions. 'The demonstration of the existence of cortical "patterns" that preserve the detail of current experience as we do in a library of many volumes is one of the first steps towards the physiology of the mind.'[13] He further said, 'The nature of the pattern, the mechanism of its formation, the mechanism of its

---

[11]Harris, T.A., *I'm OK - You're OK*, Arrow Books, 1995, p. 7.

[12]Berne, Eric, *Games People Play: The Psychology of Human Relationships*, Grove Press, 1964.

[13]Harris, T.A., *I'm OK - You're OK*, Arrow Books, p. 10.

subsequent utilization, and integrative processes that form the substratum of consciousness—these will one day be translated into physiological formulas.'[14]

Our unconscious patterns, therefore, determine a lot of what we appear to be on the surface.

In psychology, the concept of schemas is related to what Penfield found in his research. In psychology, schemas are like mental frameworks that help us make sense of our world. These schemas develop over time, based on our childhood experiences, culture and personal beliefs. They categorize information and can lead to stereotypes. They influence how we see and remember things, and make us pay more attention to information that fits our existing beliefs. They're helpful for quick judgements but can also lead to the formation of biases. They can change as we learn and adapt to new experiences. They play a big role in social interactions and can be important in therapy to address negative thought patterns.

Humans as Pattern Recognizers and Pattern Creators

Is it surprising that humans have evolved as patterned beings, pattern recognizers and pattern creators in response to our patterned world?

We respond to danger with either flight or fight, to food with salivation, to a smile with a smile, and so on. We also build patterns for our larger worldly activities—our jobs or businesses, relationships, spiritual pursuits, and so on.

Let us take a quick look at how these patterns originate, in the world external to us and within us, at all levels:

---

[14]Ibid.

1. **Our patterned universe:** Nature tends to seek order and symmetry. Many patterns arise from the tendency of systems to organize themselves in ways that minimize energy and maximize efficiency. Look at crystalline structures and symmetrical forms in biology. Our eyes, ears, noses and mouths are located closest to our brain, so that the neurological fast-moving signals emanating from these critical sense organs take the shortest time to reach our brain, and vice versa. This pattern can be found in all life forms.

   Natural systems also involve feedback loops, where the output of a process influences the input of another. These feedback loops, too, can lead to self-regulation and stability, resulting in more patterns.

   This is not a book on science. Hence, it is enough to understand that patterns are fundamental to how our universe works. We humans, too, are part of this universe and are built in the same manner.

2. **Genetic patterns:** Charles Darwin is known for his theory of evolution. He suggested that all new species arise through a gradual process of modification from earlier forms. This concept is often called 'descent with modification'.

   Darwin didn't specifically talk about the tiny details of how genes work or use the word 'patterns' in this way. He did not have a complete understanding of genetics in the modern sense, but his ideas helped set the stage for later discoveries in genetics and how traits are handed down from parents to offspring.

   Our genetic patterns are, therefore, nature's brilliant rhythm of coding the experiences of past generations into us, and for us to pass on our experiences to future generations.

3. **Involuntary patterns:** Imagine us forgetting to regulate our body temperature and dying because our bodies heat up by around 10 degrees Fahrenheit or more. Due to such a rise in our body temperature, proteins and enzymes essential for the body's functioning can denature, cells can be damaged and organs can fail! Therefore, our body's essential patterns, like regulating our body temperature, keeping our blood flowing, fighting all those germs that are incessantly attacking us, etc., all of which we need to survive, are hidden from our original and imaginative but inefficient and unreliable conscious selves. Nature makes such essential patterns almost invisible to us. They usually work very well, being unnoticed and unmonitored. That is, unless we knowingly or unknowingly disrupt them. Our modern world, for example, has disrupted a huge number of our involuntary patterns. Our digitized world has disrupted our sleep and rest, our body's repair and regeneration, the functioning of our eyes, and much more.
4. **Unconscious patterns:** During our lifetimes, more patterns get created on top of the involuntary ones as recordings at our unconscious level, based mostly on experiences in early life. These patterns act as our guidelines to shape our reactions in later life.
5. **Subconscious patterns:** We humans also voluntarily create patterns, some of which become subconscious patterns, through repetition. For example, we start learning how to drive a car with intense concentration. But as we go on practising, we begin to drive without thinking, even while talking or listening to music.

Fig. 3.1: Repeated patterns tend to become automatic, subconscious reflexes with time

Such repetitions build up physical and emotional muscles, along with the neural connections involved in these activities. With time, such patterns become almost like reflex actions, embedded in our subconscious levels.

6. **Conscious patterns:** We are always consciously trying to find and create new efficient symmetries and rhythms in our lives.

Consciousness and Patterns as Complementary Tools

Patterns help us exist—they make our lives more liveable and efficient. Without patterns, our minds, bodies, emotions and energies will always be in a state of overdrive. And our limited energies will run out due to inefficient reinterpretation of stimuli and recreation of responses throughout our lives. Will we even be able to survive under such circumstances?

Instead, while our patterns play out in the background, they free a part of our conscious and cognitive bodies, minds, emotions and energies to focus and act upon our new experiences.[15] These are experiences for which we have no genetic recordings, muscle patterns, neural pathways or emotional imprints to fall back upon. Conscious awareness and recurring patterns work in tandem to ensure our survival, perpetuate past experiences and create what did not previously exist. And they make this happen most efficiently and effectively.

Patterns and consciousness, therefore, are complementary tools. Each is incomplete without the other.

> Another confirmation of the accuracy of the concepts of consciousness and patterns comes from the development of artificial intelligence (AI). As AI is developing, the pioneers building this evolving discipline are forced to learn more about how a human being functions. This is leading to the development of AI along the twin constructs of patterns and consciousness.
>
> In the beginning, AI followed some basic, simple rules or patterns to function. However, it is gradually developing with complex-looking patterns. In addition, AI has also developed a kind of consciousness or autonomy (though within constraints) and has started to decide for itself.

Consciousness and patterns are, therefore, wonderful, essential and complementary constructs in our toolbox for survival and growth.

Let us now look more closely at how these patterns make us the powerful beings we are.

---

[15]Today, it is common knowledge that neurons also exist in parts of our bodies other than our brain. Neurons are responsible for cognition and thus, other parts of our bodies, too, are cognitive.

4

What Do Patterns Do

'It's the little details that are vital. Little things make big things happen.'

—John Wooden, American basketball coach and player

Even a basic understanding of patterns is enough to change your life. Here is a story about how patterns helped me achieve outcomes, even before I knew what exactly they were.

The year was 1972. My parents were engrossed in a deeply troubled discussion at my home in India.

The agenda of this 'parent–parent meeting' was: 'What do we do with this problem child?'

Was I really a problem child? I do not know. I was probably just another eight-year-old with his head in the clouds—except for one tiny detail. That year, as a third grader in school, I was ranked twenty-eighth in a class of 28 students. And that year was not an exception.

Now most Indian parents, especially from the middle classes, are obsessed with education. So to my parents, this situation must have felt catastrophic. It also did not help that my older brother was always at the top of his class.

During that interaction, some momentous decisions were taken. I got a hint of these when my Dad's younger brother, then a Major in the Indian Army, paid us a visit. I realized that his visit was not routine. Soon after arriving, he called me aside for a one-on-one, and delivered a long and passionate monologue.

Today, I don't recall a single word of what he said. But I clearly remember what he made me do. My uncle made me fetch my school notebook and instructed me to write there, in my own hand, 'I will come first in my class!'

I was a realist, so I bargained. 'Uncle, can we make that "third"?'

I do not remember his response, or what I finally wrote. At that point, free advice seemed to be flowing in my direction from everywhere. Another thing I clearly recall from that time is my older brother's words, 'Stop working hard, start having fun!' This was probably the best advice rendered by an eleven-year-old to an eight-year-old. He also handed me a novel by Enid Blyton—the staple diet for young Indian readers of English in those days. With this, he kicked off my lifelong love affair with books.

Also, my father, probably the behind-the-scenes director of this 'play', put me in a month-long academic 'boot camp'. But of that too, I hardly recall anything.

What I do remember is that in the next annual exam in school, for the first time in my life, I stood third in my class. For an eight-year-old, this was nothing short of a miracle.

I had little clue then as to how it happened. Maybe it was my uncle's lecture, me writing some words in a notebook, my brother's wisdom, the boot camp, the books or something else. What is important is what I inferred from this incident.

At the mere age of eight, I became convinced that if I decided something, I could do it. This conviction became an underlying pattern and it shaped everything I did from that moment onwards. What happened a few years later further reinforced this conviction.

At 16, I suddenly decided to join the National Defence Academy (NDA), an institution that prepares one to become an officer in the Indian armed forces. Maybe this was my uncle beckoning subliminally.

However, I began to question my rash decision immediately after joining. The four years of training ahead of me looked far tougher than I had imagined.

Simply put, I wanted to run away! I was not physically strong. I could neither run nor climb a rope, nor could I do most of the other mandatory physical activities. I did not play any team sports. I did not have a background in anything even remotely military.

Running away, however, would have meant loss of face. So, I began seeking solutions to make things easy and, if possible, fun for myself. I crafted one such solution for passing my 'chin-up' test. (Doing a 'chin-up' meant hanging from a thick horizontal wooden bar using your hands, hoisting your body up until your chin touched the bar and coming down till you were again in the hanging position. The academy needed us to repeat this eight times, in continuation, for it to declare that we had passed the test.)

I could not do even one proper chin-up to begin with. But I discovered that the ventilators atop our washroom cubicles were ideal for some practice. And since I was bound to visit the washroom sooner or later, I decided to insert a few quick chin-up attempts in each round to the washroom.

Fig. 4.1: Chin-ups at a washroom cubicle door

From then onwards, whenever I went to the washroom or passed by that area, I began attempting at least two chin-ups, once while entering and next while leaving. Each attempt took just a few seconds.

In the beginning, I couldn't manage even one proper chin-up. However, with time, it became easier. Pretty soon, I started utilizing every opportunity I got to practise the chin-ups.

It almost became a subconscious reflex for me. I do not recall investing massive effort in the exercise. Instead, I started enjoying feeling fit. Soon, I overcame the minimum required standard of eight chin-ups, then went past 12, 16 and beyond.

Many similar pattern-crafting opportunities surfaced in the academy. I just inserted these tiny 'rhythms' into the tightly structured routines that comprised our lives as cadets. Each one of these rhythms just needed some initial head-scratching. Since those were tiny and fun anyway, I started following them.

I had no grand plans. At the time, I was simply working to survive those four years.

Our military history textbooks were heavy and boring. So, I leveraged my love for stories, reading and watching movies, and went through many amazing books and movies dealing with stories of the military, like *The Young Carthaginian*, *The Desert Fox*, *The Duellists*, *Apocalypse Now*, *A Bridge Too Far*, and so on.

Soon, this habit of mine turned into such an abiding interest in military history that even our prescribed texts, like Carl von Clausewitz's *On War*, started seeming easy and interesting to read.

I started practising the nunchaku, an East Asian martial arts routine, to strengthen my upper body (still love it); drew charts to memorize details; practised speed-writing; learnt to sleep at a moment's notice (still can); and taught myself how to switch my mind off whenever any senior was yelling his head off at me!

Four years later, by the time I graduated—practically without realizing it or aiming for it—I had reached the top of my batch, winning the president's gold medal, without feeling that I had to make any significant effort in the process.

I had somehow stumbled upon the secret to achieving goals. At the time, I defined it as creating tiny routines that were enjoyable and repeating them till they became subconscious reflexes. I had not discovered anything new. I had only learnt to manipulate simple things and build routines.

You also know, by now, that this was but a partial ignorant peek, like looking through a keyhole into the immensely powerful world of tiny, conscious patterns within and around us.

The anecdotes above show how powerful tiny conscious patterns can be. Here are some common outcomes of patterns that you can apply to every area of your life.

Fig. 4.2: What chaos looks like: a pile of scattered bricks

You have seen the pile of bricks in the illustration above; the same bricks can look very different when patterned.

Table 4.1
What Patterns Do

Patterns bring order to a chaotic world. They simplify things.	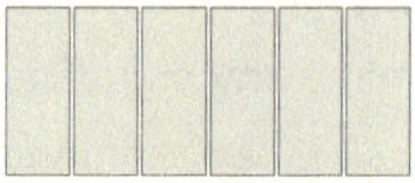
You can organize, quantify and control patterned things. Repetitive patterns become powerful resources to use as you wish.	
Patterns are energy-efficient.	
Patterns make us creative.	
Patterns help us identify beauty in simplicity.	
Patterns help us create incredibly complex things; thus, they open up limitless possibilities.	
Patterns lead to conscious awareness; there can be no awareness without patterns.	
Patterns enable balance, self-mastery and success.	

Let us see how you can use conscious patterns in your lives.

Patterns Beat Chaos

Sam and Anita were out partying with friends till late in the night. At the party, Sam couldn't stop thinking about the upcoming meeting at work the next day. The moment they returned, he quickly scribbled down some points for that meeting before crashing on bed. The next morning, on Monday, he woke up late and had to skip his morning exercise routine. He dressed quickly and ended up nicking his chin while shaving. Cursing, he grabbed a toast and jumped into his car. Anita had already left for work by then.

Stuck in traffic, Sam controlled the urge to honk at the car ahead. As soon as he reached his office, he ran inside, forcing himself into the crowded lift, inviting glares.

He got to his cabin and opened his briefcase. 'Damn!' he swore, realizing that he had forgotten the scribbled sheet at his bedside. He began to quickly list those points again for the meeting.

The morning went past in a tizzy, playing catch-up. A client meeting consumed an hour from Sam's packed schedule. He ended up skipping lunch, and had to grab a coffee and doughnut instead. He knew this would churn his innards, but he was too busy to care!

The remaining day was equally chaotic for him.

He left from work at five in the evening and, by the time he was home, he was too exhausted to even talk to Anita. He just collapsed on the couch, and with glazed eyes, began surfing the TV channels in an attempt to give himself some rest.

Though I hope not, this could well be a day from your life. But with just a little conscious effort to use different patterns, Sam's day could have been quite different, like the one below.

Sam and Anita were out partying with friends till late. But before leaving for the party, Sam had prepared for the next day. He always planned for his next day.

Anyway, it was late by the time Sam went to bed. But the next morning, he stuck to his routine of waking up on time. He woke up a little groggy, but by the time he was through with his morning routine and exercises, he felt fit as a fiddle. As always, he left early for work to beat the morning traffic. He had selected an accommodation closer to his company, so the drive to the office would not take too long. By then, Anita had already left for work.

Sam reached the office and, as was his routine, started work early. By the time the others clocked in, he had already gone through most of the work piled up for Monday. Going forward, the client meeting would have consumed an hour extra had his executive assistant not popped in at the right time, as briefed, to remind him that there was another task lined up. The meeting was quickly wrapped up and a follow-up call was fixed with the client to cover what all could not be discussed in the meeting.

After a relaxed lunch, which he made sure to never skip, Sam dealt with some unexpected developments with ease, for he always counted in extra time for such tasks. Before leaving the office, he had his executive assistant chart out his next day in detail.

Sam left the office at 4.45 p.m., just before peak traffic kicked in. When he reached home, he felt fairly fresh, and eagerly waited for Anita to return. He had lots to discuss with her.

Does the above sound like fiction? It is. But it is not too far from a possible reality. Successful and happy people make sure to add the element of routine to their daily lives and seize control of events.

Our patterns also shape our environment. Place a huge boulder in a stream and soon we will find the stream flowing around it. Our environment, too, begins to behave predictably and to adjust itself in response to consciously created patterns. We also adjust ourselves according to the things that we cannot reshape.

The opposite is also true. If we do not control our environment, it will control us. There are many who are always confused owing to the fact that their environment is too chaotic.

Patterns Support Creativity

There is this absurd notion that creativity is incompatible with any form of routine (or discipline, if you will), and that to have one, the other must be let go of.

The truth is exactly the opposite. Patterns help us become more creative, by helping us create longer, more frequent and efficient periods and spaces for our minds to explore.

Erik Wahl, a well-known American graffiti artist, speed-painter, author, motivational speaker and entrepreneur, says, 'The paradox of creativity is that structure creates freedom. I am a naturally creative spirit who has built my business with extreme orderliness and attention to detail. The strength of this structure gives me greater confidence and freedom to create.'[16]

Wahl lists examples of known masters who used patterns to support their creativity.

---

[16]'Discipline of Creativity', *Eric Wahl,* https://tinyurl.com/2huzmnsw. Accessed on 11 March 2024.

- Beethoven would sit down at daybreak each day, whatever the season, and compose music until 3.00 p.m.
- Kafka would begin writing at 11.30 p.m. without fail.
- Mozart would teach during the day and compose in the evenings.
- Picasso would have lunch with his family in silence every day, and only allowed visitors once a week.

Wahl adds: 'When fanatical discipline is combined with empirical creativity, the challenges of mental fatigue and mind-blocks are no match in the pursuit of excellence. The only things these individuals have in common is the rigidity of their daily routines, carving out the pockets of quietude to listen to their inner creative voice.'[17]

He concludes with this advice: 'Until you and I build up the capacity to focus like the masters, let us begin by adhering to the cheeky mindset of Peter De Vries…"I write when I'm inspired, and I see to it that I'm inspired at nine o'clock every morning."'

Creativity without discipline is like a river without banks. It can be dangerous.

Patterns also underlie every original creation. A great painting is not mere brush strokes applied to a canvas. A great artist first masters the basic patterns or principles that underlie every great painting. Then they apply those patterns consciously to create an original masterpiece. A business owner, too, masters the fundamental patterns of their business to create something new.

---

[17]Ibid.

Tiny Repetitive Patterns Lead to Success

Consider these questions:

- How much could a little change in your posture improve your fitness? How much could a few but frequent push-ups strengthen your arms?
- How much effect could tiny adjustments to your approximately 22,000 breaths, 100,000 heartbeats and thousands of thoughts daily have on your outcomes?
- How much could little changes in how you eat, drink and sleep affect all your outcomes?
- How sharp could your memory become if you start reviewing your day before going to bed each night?
- How much could a smile and a few kind words alter your relationships?
- Could honing your basic motor, mental and emotional skills alter all your outcomes at work?
- Could tiny adjustments to how you manage your complex job, business, finances, relationships and leisure activities affect the outcomes?
- Could perpetual clarity about your past and future make your present amazing?

The effects of aligned patterns when repeated incessantly are not additive but exponential.

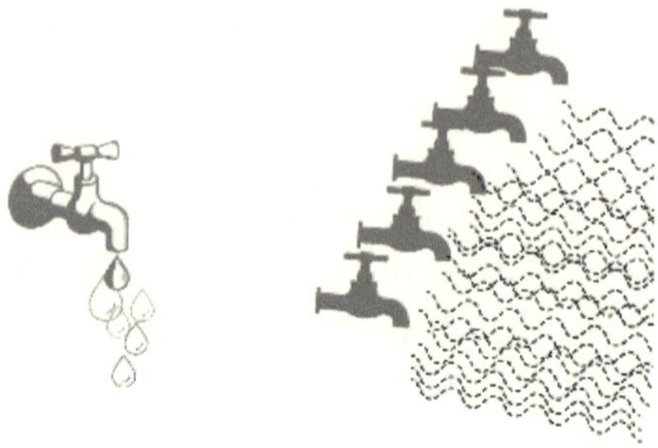

Fig. 4.3: Tiny incessant patterns, when consciously aligned together towards a common outcome, become immensely powerful

Consider the example of a person who has high self-worth. The one pattern (high self-worth) affects an entire layer of their higher level patterns, like self-confidence, sociability and leadership. Each one of these patterns further affects another higher layer of patterns, like the ability to address others, the ability to listen, to learn, and so on. How they take difficult decisions, lead others, manage their finances, relationships, passions, etc., are all ceaselessly powered by that single underlying pattern, which is their high self-worth.

The book, *The Blue Zones: 9 Lessons for Living Longer From the People Who've Lived the Longest*, by Dan Buettner, a National Geographic Fellow and journalist, explores the lifestyles and habits of communities where people tend to live exceptionally long and healthy lives.[18] Dan identified common patterns amongst these communities:

[18]Buettner, Dan, *The Blue Zones: Lessons for Living Longer from the People Who've Lived the Longest*, National Geographic Society, 2010.

- Plant-based diets
- Moderate caloric intake
- Physical activity
- Social engagement
- Giving importance to family and community
- Purpose in life derived from work, family or community involvement

Hal Elrod, in his book *The Miracle Morning*, introduces the concept of a morning routine that includes activities like meditation, affirmations, visualization, exercise, reading and writing. Elrod proposes that starting our day with positive and intentional habits can transform our life.

In the book *Atomic Habits*, the author James Clear provides examples from his own life and from the lives of others about how tiny and positive changes in our habits can lead to significant changes in our lives.

Not just habits, but all patterns within and around us—our environment, genetics, bodies, minds, emotions, actions, etc.—play a huge role in our success.

Such patterns and routines can be spotted in the lives of several successful people.

- Benjamin Franklin, the most accomplished American of his age, shortlisted frugality, humility and sincerity along with 10 other virtues to concentrate upon in his life. Thereafter, he focussed on one of these virtues for a week, covering all of them in 13 weeks, four times each year!

- Mark Zuckerberg, CEO of Facebook, always wears the same type and colour of T-shirt. Tiny patterns like these help him reduce unnecessary decision-making and allow him to focus on the things that he cares about in life.
- Michael Phelps, with eight Gold Medals in the 2008 Olympics, says, 'It's just hitting those little milestones, no matter what it is.'[19]
- Mahatma Gandhi exhibited many steady routines, like writing, fasting, reading and public service.

Patterns Enable Success Along with Self-Mastery and Fulfilment

American author and motivational speaker Zig Ziglar said: 'I believe that being successful means having a balance of success stories across the many areas of your life. You can't truly be considered successful in your business life if your home life is in shambles.'

There are certain essential factors in life, like our health, mental faculties, work, relationships, basic finances and personal goals in which we cannot afford to fail, irrespective of our mastery over other things.

Albert Einstein had a brilliant mind. Yet, his personal life was not enviable. His wife had left him in 1914. His health had been failing him. He died at the age of 76. He probably lasted that long only because he followed his pattern of daily walks to work and back.

[19]Martin, Emmie, '23-Time Gold Medalist Michael Phelps Uses a Simple Trick to Stay Focused on His Goals', *Make It*, 1 January 2019, https://tinyurl.com/2w36269f. Accessed on 20 May 2024.

> V.G. Siddhartha, the founder and owner of Café Coffee Day (CCD), tragically died by suicide in July 2019. Siddhartha's tragic death was a significant blow to the business community in India, and prompted reflections on the pressures and struggles faced by entrepreneurs, even those who appear successful on the surface.

This book aims at helping you achieve success in all significant areas of life. It also aims at helping you achieve self-mastery and a sense of fulfilment in all moments. Focussing on tiny patterns will help you retain balance in all essential areas of life. Forming conscious patterns will help you master tiny root patterns, achieve self-mastery and help lead a good life. Success is the natural by-product of living life well.

Our patterns enable us to enjoy good health, clarity, joy, creativity, fulfilment, and so much more.

There are several limitless assets that we can deploy to our benefit:

- Good health, a clear mind and controlled emotions
- Healthy relationships, financial stability and a job that one loves
- Self-mastery and fulfilment
- Wealth, which may be defined as the sum total of all the assets including the ones listed above

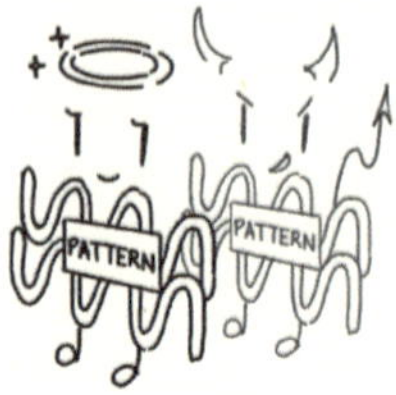

5

The Paradox of Unconscious Patterns

'Until you make the unconscious conscious,
it will direct your life and you will call it fate.'

—Carl Jung, psychologist

There is a flip side to patterns. We need to understand it, so that we may deal with it.

Most of our patterns give us immense power. However, some patterns can harm us and hold us back till the time we become conscious of them and deal with them. Such patterns exist everywhere—in our environment and our genetic, involuntary, unconscious, subconscious and conscious levels.

Our Environmental Patterns

Our environment is everything outside us—animate and inanimate, what we can observe and what we cannot. It is our environment that created us and not the other way around. It has a huge impact on us. Those who ignore their environment play one-sided chess.

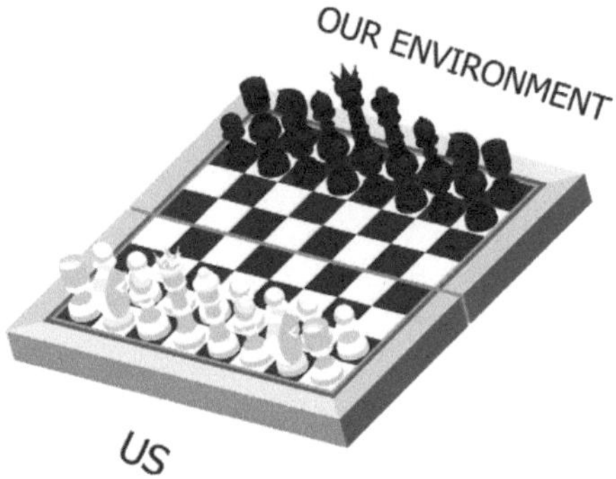

Fig. 5.1: We need to consider every 'move' of our environment and play the game of life accordingly, by making our own moves

Our environment is neutral. It is neither specifically for us nor against us. We humans, like all other species, were created to be aligned with our natural environment. But a paradox arises because we humans often assume that our environment was created for us; we assume that we humans are central to it. This assumption makes us forget that we cannot control everything in our environment. We forget that our environment can even destroy us, as it is powerful. We take our environment for granted, forgetting how to work in tandem with it.

So, as individuals, we must figure out what works for us in our environment and what does not. For example, our environment could be enabling, but many patterns in our environment could also be restrictive, unsuitable, disorganized, disabling, discouraging, and so on. Our job is to recognize which patterns will work for us and which ones will not.

We must understand what we can control in our environment and what we cannot. We must use what we are aligned with. We must reshape what we can control, if needed. And we must realign ourselves with what we cannot control.

Many people complain about their environment but never bother to do anything about it. To a large extent, our environment is our choice.

Our Genetic and Involuntary Patterns

Genetic and involuntary patterns are largely built to work for us, but even these can harm us.

For example, genes related to insulin resistance evolved in our ancestors thousands of years ago during the Ice Age and periods when food was scarce. Those genes gave our ancestors a huge advantage and helped them survive. However, those same genetic characteristics can make us diabetic in today's time.

> The Tarahumara people, of the Copper Canyon region of northern Mexico, have a tradition of running long distances, sometimes exceeding 200 or 300 km, as part of religious and cultural events. Their metabolisms have been shaped for such extreme exertion over the ages. But when the same people are exposed to modern lifestyle practises, like sedentary living and fast food, they gain weight more readily than other communities. Mexico has one of the highest obesity rates in the world.

It is important to understand such genetic predispositions. Once we know about them, we can look for ways to deal with them.

Similarly, some of our involuntary patterns can also cause problems. If I am exposed to a cold draft, especially directed towards my head, I get severe migraine. This happens due to vasoconstriction. This is involuntary constriction in blood vessels in the skin, reducing blood flow to the head and neck, resulting in a migraine. Of course, my body does this involuntarily, to reduce heat loss from my head and neck.

There are other such paradoxical involuntary patterns that could harm us. It is important to understand them.

Our Unconscious Patterns

Do you recall Dr Penfield's experiments, in which he discovered past experiences and emotional patterns embedded in patients' unconscious minds? Many such patterns can be destructive for us today.

Suppose a child is in a non-conducive environment, with an unsympathetic parent, or is growing up in a war zone. As Dr Penfield's experiments show us, such a child would develop unconscious patterns to survive in that environment. But those patterns might harm that child later in life.

But why do such harmful patterns get created in the first place?

The answer is simple. When a child learns the pattern of fear while responding to an aggressive adult, that fear is not harmful. That fear is extremely useful to the child at that time. A five-year-old needs to be afraid of a powerful, aggressive grown-up. It helps them run away!

However, having the same pattern of fear 20 years later might harm the person. Despite being an adult, they might fear their boss, just because the latter happens to be an aggressive authority figure, similar to the abusive adult in their past.

There are several other examples that can demonstrate

how a single significant event of the past can create negative patterns.

Take the example of a kid who falls flat on his face while attempting something new in sports class. His classmates laugh at him. The humiliation associated with that incident gets cemented in his mind. It blocks him from trying anything new later in life, perhaps forever.

Such negative patterns can get created even due to sheer habit or repetition of the past event. A grown-up elephant remains tied to a stake with a flimsy rope. It never tries to break that rope since it could not break it as a baby. It remains psychologically bound to its past experience of helplessness.

We must understand such harmful patterns.

Patterns of our ego or our self-image are amongst the most powerful and sometimes the most destructive. Most adults have the personality 'I'm not okay, you're okay'. They secretly consider themselves inferior to others, and this affects their personality and performance. Getting rid of such a pattern is necessary.

> In the book *Games People Play: The Basic Handbook of Transactional Analysis*, the author Eric Berne explains how all of us adopt 'positions' in our lives and play 'games' to reinforce our beliefs about ourselves. We grow so comfortable with our familiar defeating patterns that we cling desperately to them.
>
> A victim tries to manoeuvre into a position of victimhood. People who are convinced that they are not capable of succeeding find the responsibilities that go with success uncomfortable and frightening. They wriggle out of situations that could lead to their success! They find familiarity, comfort and safety in sticking to their past patterns that lead to their failure and mediocrity.

Many of our unconscious patterns, therefore, carry powerful blueprints for our own failures.

Here is a simple rule of thumb to identify unconscious patterns: If an action, emotion or thought kicks in even before one's analytical brain analyses it, one is in the grip of an unconscious pattern.

This is why evolution, which gave us powerful patterns, also gave us a powerful consciousness. If our past patterns become meaningless or counterproductive, our consciousness is meant to find and remove those patterns. Nature gives us a powerful instinctive intelligence that tells us what is right and what is wrong, provided we allow ourselves to listen to it.

In Layers (parts) II and III of the book, you will learn how to dig out and remove or modify your regressive past patterns and to consciously create useful ones.

Our Subconscious and Conscious Harmful Patterns

There are many subconscious and conscious patterns that harm us. Though we seem to be partially or fully conscious of them, I still call them unconscious patterns because we are not aware of their negative effects.

> In the book *Blink*, author Malcolm Gladwell provides an interesting example. A psychologist named John M. Gottiman video-recorded discussions between volunteer married couples while they were talking about some minor matters on which they disagreed. These were not violent disagreements but minor ones, many of them even banal, like whether they should adopt a dog.

Gottiman then analysed and labelled each second of such interactions. He found that by analysing all one-second snippets from an hour-long conversation between the couple, he could predict with 95 per cent accuracy whether they would still be married 15 years later.

He also found that by reducing the length of each recording to 15 minutes, the success rate of his predictions dropped only to 90 per cent. Gottiman's fellow professor, Sybil Carrere, went further. He found that by analysing any three minutes of any such interaction, he could still predict fairly accurately whether that couple would be divorced later in life.

This is what was actually happening. Those couples were actually repeatedly displaying certain facial micro-expressions during their interactions. Gottiman and his colleagues made their predictions based on an analysis of those facial expressions. Couples likely to divorce later in life revealed contempt for one another in their micro-expressions.

The couples in question were, almost certainly, not even aware that they were heading for a divorce, say 15 years later. Their outward laughter, banter and friendly disagreements gave no clue either to them, or to a casual observer, unless the observer was trained and knew what to look for. This means that while being dimly aware of contempt for the other, each partner gave hardly any weight to that feeling.[20]

Imagine such a couple trying hard to be nice to each other, and wondering why their marriage was still falling apart!

[20]Gladwell, Malcolm, *Blink: The Power Of Thinking Without Thinking,* Penguin UK, 2006, p. 12.

We are more blind to our patterns than we think. Why is this so? Most of the time, this is due to a lack of awareness and knowledge.

For example, a person might be pretty bad at a certain skill and be quite unaware of it. They might be an average singer stuck with the belief that they have a great voice. Or they might be a jealous and resentful person but convince themself that they are accommodating and caring.

The funny thing is that others can usually instantly spot many such patterns in us, but we might still remain unaware of the same.

There are patterns that we know are bad for us, like smoking, drinking, consuming drugs, binge surfing, breaking commitments (professional and personal), etc. In most instances, we are unable to get rid of such patterns.

Paradoxical Patterns about Our Past and Future

Many people carry the patterns they form in their past—most of which are totally irrelevant for them in the present time. If a person was poor in the past, they might behave like a pauper today even though they are wealthy, or they might show off their wealth to overcome their feeling of inferiority.

Similarly, when people imagine a great future, they become happy and hopeful. But when they envision bleak days ahead, they are driven to depression and suffering, all because of a future that might not even come about!

Such patterns harm us. We must weed them out.

Intent versus Actions

Amongst the most powerful paradoxical patterns that hold the seeds to destroy us are our patterns of intent.

Suppose a person says, with absolutely genuine intent:

'I am a learner. That's my most important trait.'

'My parents are my first priority.'

'I never grow angry with my employees. They are like my wards.'

'I am a giver. I give of myself each day.'

All these are patterns of intent and all of these are futile unless they are accompanied by matching patterns of action.

Let us analyse the patterns of action of the above individual and see where they lead them.

Table 5.1

People's Actions Often Do Not Match Their Intentions

Patterns of Intent or Self-Image	**Patterns of Action**	**Calculating Outcomes over 1 Year**	**Outcomes over 1 Year**
'I am a learner. That's my most important trait.'	Things learnt today / on most days = 0 / nearly zero	Nearly zero hours × 365 = nearly zero hours spent on learning in a year	Total learning = nearly zero
'My parents are my first priority.'	Time given to parents each week = 0.5 hours	0.5 × 52 = 26 hours	Effort on relationship with parents = low

'I never grow angry with my employees. They are like my wards.'	Loses temper almost every alternate day = nearly thrice a week	3 × 52 = 156 times	Anger at work = extremely high
'I am a giver. I give of myself each day.'	Perhaps gives once every quarter	1 × 4 quarters = 4 times	Giving = negligible

Patterns of intent are conscious and we believe in them. Our intentions fool us into believing that they are our actions, whereas these two are very different things. Ultimately, actions matter way more than intentions. Intentions without actions are of little value.

In the other parts of the book, we will see what all can be done about the patterns that harm us.

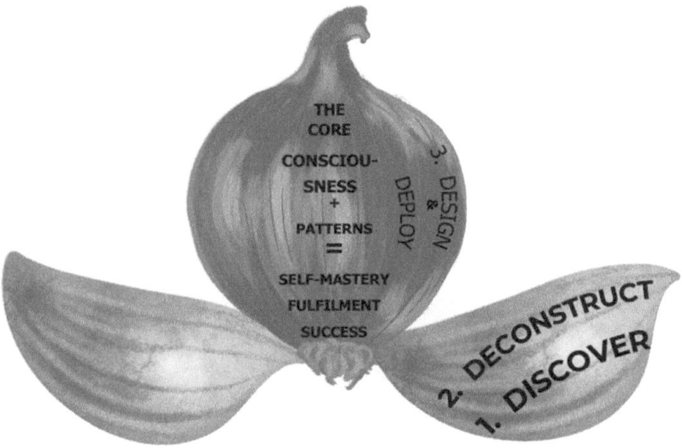

Layer II: Deconstruct Your Patterns

'To be willing is only half the job.'

—Armenian proverb

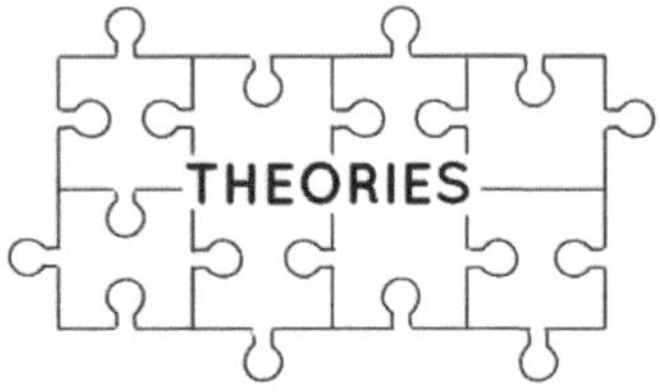

6

Existing Habit Theories

'There is a distinction, but no opposition, between theory and practice. Each to a certain extent supposes the other. Theory is dependent on practice; practice must have preceded theory.'

—Sir William Hamilton,
Ninth Baronet, Scottish metaphysician and philosopher

Before getting to deconstructing and demystifying patterns to understand their root causes, let us look at some wonderful work already done in the field of habits, which are a subset of human patterns.

The Cue–Routine–Reward Cycle

Let us understand this with the help of an example:

- Cue: A woman in a supermarket spots a chocolate. That chocolate becomes the 'cue' or 'trigger' that sets off her craving.

- Routine: She buys the chocolate and eats it.
- Reward: She feels good while eating the chocolate.
- Over time, she begins to anticipate the taste of the chocolate as soon as she sees it or even thinks about it. The craving for the reward begins to appear as soon as she spots the cue.
- In time, eating chocolate turns into a habit for her. As a result, she becomes overweight.

Charles Duhigg uses this 'cue–routine–reward cycle' to explain habitual behaviours in his wonderful book *The Power of Habit.*[21] He writes that this cue–routine–reward cycle repeats itself till it turns into a habit.

Therefore, we can control our habits by understanding and controlling our responses to cues. For example, the woman could have started carrying an apple to ward off the temptation of eating chocolate.

It is important to understand that cues create strong cravings that are difficult to overcome. Besides, we cannot remove all cues. We cannot tell the entire world to stop offering chocolate to the woman as cues. That is the problem with external cues.

When the woman sees a chocolate, perhaps she forgets about the apple and automatically reacts by buying and eating the chocolate. Most probably, the woman is later bewildered by her own action as she does not want to gain weight! Perhaps, every time she gives in, she promises herself to never give in again to her cravings for chocolate. Yet, she fails to understand why she cannot stop her cravings,

[21]Duhigg, Charles, *The Power of Habit: Why We Do What We Do in Life and Business*, Random House, 2012.

even though she knows that she will hate herself later! But the woman's actions are mere scripted responses, with little conscious control, like a puppet being pulled by strings!

Fogg's Behaviour Model

Dr B.J. Fogg, founder of the Behaviour Design Lab at Stanford University, suggested a solution to tackle the problem of cues. Fogg linked motivation, ability and prompts (or what Duhigg called cues). The Fogg Behaviour Model (FBM) says that for prompts to succeed, both motivation and ability must be available in the right quantities.[22]

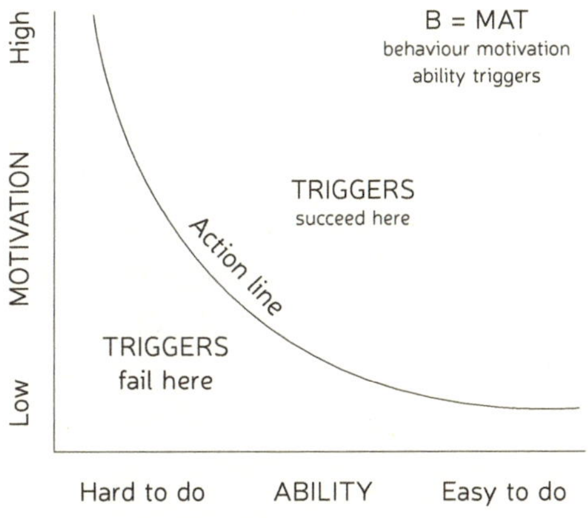

Fig. 6.1: Fogg's Behaviour Model

For example, consider a woman who wants to run. She watches someone running and that acts as a prompt for her also to run:

---

[22] 'Fogg Behaviour Model', *Stanford | Behavior Design Lab*, https://tinyurl.com/b8x7yns7. Accessed on 12 March 2024.

- If both her motivation (inner drive) and her ability (skill) to run are high, then the prompt will work. She will run.
- If her motivation is high but the ability is low, she can still drive herself to run.
- If her motivation is low but the ability is high, she can still run due to her ability alone.
- If her motivation and ability both are low, the prompt will fail.

To overcome this, Fogg suggested adopting tiny habits. If the levels of both motivation and ability needed to do something are small, accomplishing the task becomes a lot easier. James Clear's wonderful book, *Atomic Habits,* too suggests this approach.

This method is so powerful. My two-chin-ups-at-a-time pattern succeeded because doing just two chin-ups at a time needed little motivation and ability.

A corollary to this could be that if one can generate the required motivation and ability to do things, one can create habits at will.

But what do you do in cases where this still does not work? For example, a retired senior executive I know wanted to lose weight. But he did not succeed, even though he placed cues, tried practising on a smaller scale, and so on. He could not sustain those activities for a significant period of time in order for them to make a difference. Obviously, he was missing something.

Other Behavioural Theories

Behavioural scientists have proposed many theories for habit formation and change. I have listed key behaviour change theories on my website.[23] Of these, the *Biopsychosocial Model* is a comprehensive model that considers biological, psychological and social factors that influence behaviour, including habit formation and change.

However, comparing any of these models to the concept of patterns is a little tricky because patterns are not just about behaviours. They are not even found only in humans; they are all around us and within us.

But I have found that all these models fit perfectly within an overall construct of conscious patterns. I believe this is what makes the technique of conscious patterns so universally applicable.

---

[23]'Existing Habit Theories', *Sunil Prem*, 17 March 2024, https://tinyurl.com/253epxv7. Accessed on 15 April 2024.

7

How Patterns Are Formed

'...under the turmoil of chaos and change, there is a beauty of patterns and designs.'

—Amit Ray,
author of *Mindfulness Meditation for Corporate Leadership and Management*

We will start our analysis of patterns at the macro level. We will end it at micro level, and by then you will come to understand how tiny patterns work. This is the level at which you will learn to apply tiny patterns consciously to achieve your outcomes.

Patterns in the Larger Scheme of Things

Let us analyse how our conscious patterns are related to the universe at the largest level.

Consider a honey bee that hops from one flower to another. As it does so, pollen from those flowers sticks to the bee and goes with it to other plants. The bee is hopping from one flower to another to look for food. Unbeknownst to the bee, it is also helping plants exchange pollen and reproduce. If all bees, and other pollinators like butterflies, moths, birds, bats, etc., were to die, then all those plants would die, too.

Like the bee, we humans also serve a deeper purpose and are partners with our universe, whether we realize it or not. Our basic biological and safety needs and our need for love, belongingness and esteem seem to exist to drive our ultimate urge of self-actualization. We try to do this by expressing our capabilities to the fullest and, in the process, aid our universe in its march towards increasing complexity and beauty.

Now compare what we do to what John F. Haught, Emeritus Professor of Theology at Georgetown University, says about our evolving universe:

> In view of the discoveries of sciences ranging from astrophysics to biology, today there can be little doubt, at least when we view it over the long run, that the universe has wended its way directionally from simplicity to complexity, from triviality to more intense versions of ordered novelty—that is, toward emergent beauty.[24]

And this is where our patterns and our consciousness fit in the larger scheme. Our patterns and our consciousness help us move from simplicity to complexity, from triviality to more intense versions of ordered novelty, that is, towards emergent beauty.

My aim here is to show you how profoundly relevant our conscious patterns are even to our highest pursuits, as

---

[24]Haught, John, 'What Is the Purpose of Existence?', *Engelsberg Ideas*, 11 August 2020, https://tinyurl.com/bded2vx8. Accessed on 20 May 2024.

individuals, as a species and as an entire universe that moves in a particular direction.

With this, let us get back to analysing conscious patterns at individual level.

How Cycles of Patterns Get Created

> Remember Sam from the previous chapter? One day, he was just about to reach home from work. As he turned his car towards his home, he noticed some flowers in a shop across the road from him.
>
> *Why don't I buy some flowers for Anita?* he thought. That thought made him feel warm all over.
>
> He quickly drove over and bought a beautiful bunch of flowers. At home, as soon as he surprised Anita with the flowers, she gave him a big hug. He felt glad about his decision to buy flowers for her.

This is how humans behave consciously. The following figure explains the cycle of conscious behaviour.

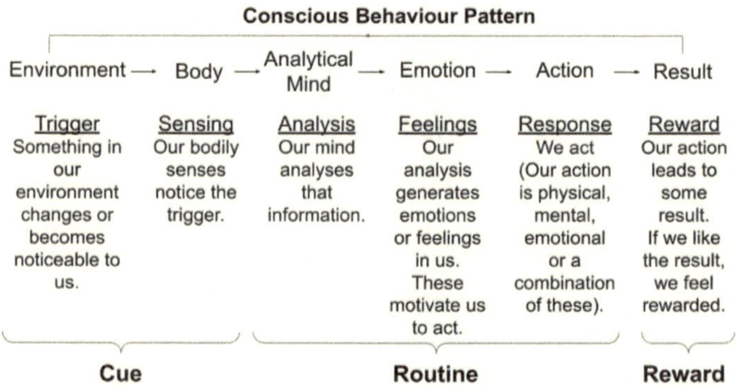

Fig. 7.1: The cycle of conscious human behaviour

As depicted in the diagram, this cycle is similar to Charles Duhigg's cue–routine–reward cycle mentioned in the previous chapter. Only the terminologies differ.

If we repeat this cycle often, it will turn into a pattern. For example, when a salesperson follows a sales technique repetitively, it turns into their conscious selling pattern.

Such conscious patterns are extremely useful. But in the previous chapter we also saw a woman who sees a chocolate, develops a craving, buys and eats it; she does this repeatedly every time she sees the cue (the chocolate). This turns into a habit and makes her overweight. So, the wrong conscious patterns can also harm us.

Some of these patterns turn into a routine, hence becoming part of subconscious patterns. Driving is one such example.

Such subconscious patterns are the 'holy grail' of the technique of conscious patterns, as they are effortless and let us continue other activities in parallel. For example, we can think or talk (conscious activities) while walking (subconscious activity).

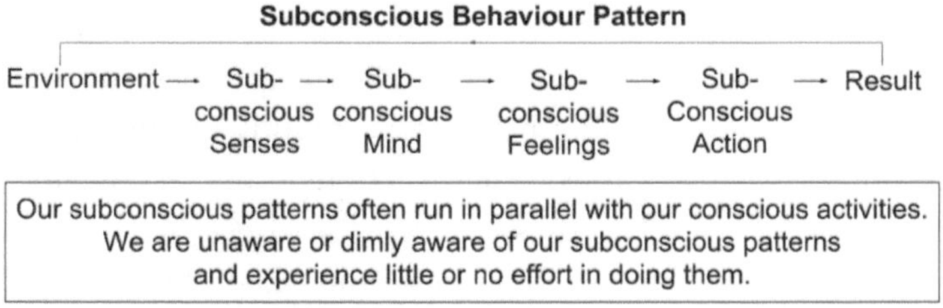

Fig. 7.2: The cycle of subconscious behaviour

Wrong subconscious patterns, like slouching while working (poor posture), can also harm us.

Unconscious Behaviour Pattern

Environment → Filtered Senses → Unconscious Mind → Unconscious Feelings → Unconscious Actions → Result

Our unconscious patterns bypass our analytical mind. Instead, our unconscious mind, which holds our past recordings, takes over. We simply replay and relive our past thoughts, feelings and actions.

Fig. 7.3: The cycle of unconscious behaviour

We also build unconscious patterns, most of which help us. For example, we unconsciously follow rules of right and wrong, safety and security that we learnt during our childhood. But the wrong unconscious patterns can harm us. In an earlier chapter, we saw how a child ill-treated by a parent starts becoming fearful and replays that behaviour later in life.

Similarly, we also build involuntary and genetic patterns. Our involuntary patterns are extremely useful but not always. For example, while speaking in public, we may begin to tremble involuntarily, affecting our performance.

As a child, I suffered from severe motion sickness. I would throw up while travelling on a winding road. But once I got deployed in the army, I travelled everywhere in every sort of vehicle, including helicopters, circling around during reconnaissance missions. After such repeated exposures, I overcame my travel sickness.

Hence, involuntary patterns, too, can be changed. Breathing is the key physical channel through which we can control our mind, emotions, heartbeat, pulse rate and other involuntary systems.

Likewise, our genetic patterns, too, get shaped in the same manner. Research has shown that a pregnant woman with a diet high in fat and sugar may predispose her future child to metabolic disorders, like obesity, type 2 diabetes or cardiovascular diseases later in life, even if those children have a healthy diet themselves. But a pregnant woman can avoid this possibility by modifying her diet. Therefore, our genetic expressions, too, are controllable.

Variations to Cycles of Human Behaviour

> Anita was driving back home after a class reunion. It had been a lovely evening. After meeting her former schoolmates, she was in a mellow mood.
>
> *Everyone has really aged,* she thought to herself, and leant forward to turn on the radio.
>
> And as she looked up, she saw a fawn standing in the middle of the road, frozen with fear. In an instant, her foot slammed down on the brake as her hands swerved the steering. The car skidded sideways, missed the deer narrowly, crashed into the fence and screeched along before coming to a halt.
>
> With heightened awareness, Anita saw the fawn dart away and disappear into the trees.
>
> It was minutes before she could call up her partner in a shaking voice.

The pattern creation cycles get modified according to the situation.

In this example, Anita instantly switches from her subconscious driving behaviour to applying brakes without conscious thought (unconscious behaviour). Her brain kicks in with pre-scripted moves. She also becomes hyper-aware, with her eyes (senses) narrowing to notice only the object that matters (the fawn), ignoring everything else. Her heartbeat rises (involuntary behaviour) and her body becomes tense, ready for action. Her analytical mind kicks in last.

Further, all the cycles in the figures above are shown as starting due to an environmental cue. However, any step along the cycle could trigger it, that is, an environmental cue, a change in our body, a thought, an emotion or an action.

These cycles can also skip steps. For example, we saw earlier that neurons also exist in various body parts. So, our bodies too know how to react directly, especially in response to environmental cues.

Our Micro-Patterns

The larger patterns consist of many smaller patterns within our environment, bodies, minds, emotions and actions. For example, while following a certain pattern for selling, salespersons create smaller patterns in their environment (physical and social), bodies, minds, emotions and actions. Together, these smaller patterns make up the bigger sales pattern.

We must focus on these smaller patterns. These are much simpler to analyse and use. With larger patterns, we can get lost in their complexity.

Stressors Affecting our Micro-Patterns

We have seen that many of our patterns can be flawed. The causes of these flaws are usually our stressors.

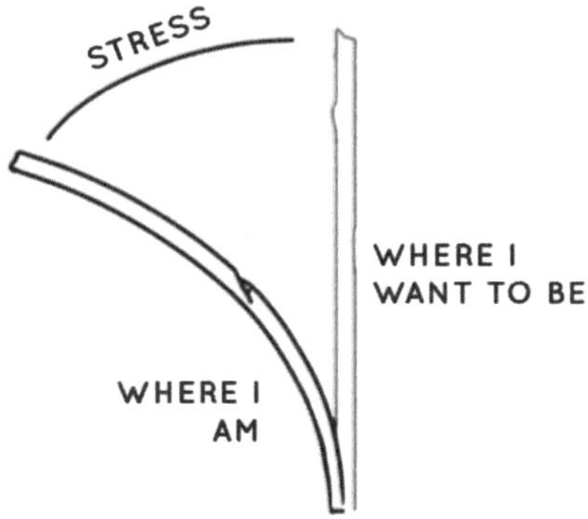

Fig. 7.4: Stress is the tension that arises within us as a result of the conflict between where we are versus where we want to be

Stressors are external or internal events that can trigger the body's stress response, leading to physical, mental, emotional and behavioural reactions. These stressors can vary widely and affect people differently. Here are some common types of stressors:

1. **External stressors**
   (a) **Environmental stressors:** These include factors in our physical environment, such as pollution, overcrowding and extreme weather conditions.
   (b) **Psychosocial stressors:** These can also include social factors, including work-related stress and daily hassles, relationship or work conflicts, discrimination, social isolation, peer pressure, financial difficulties, major life events like divorce or loss of a loved one, and so on.
2. **Internal stressors**
   (a) **Physiological or biological stressors:** These can be internal factors, such as bodily or hormonal imbalances (like being overweight), ageing, genetic

predispositions, medical conditions, illnesses, injuries or chronic pain.

(b) **Mental or cognitive stressors:** Stress can also result from cognitive factors, such as lack of knowledge or analytical abilities, cognitive load, complexity of tasks, uncertainty, difficult choices or dilemmas, negative thought patterns, boredom or excessive worry, unbalanced ego states and unrealistic expectations. Stressors are also caused by our past recordings, which we refer to as our beliefs, like lack of self-worth.

(c) **Emotional stressors:** Emotional factors like anxiety, fear, anger, shame and sorrow can contribute to stress when they are prolonged or intense.

(d) **Activity-induced stressors:** Factors like poor physical health and well-being lead to fatigue.

While some of these stressors might be obvious, others might be hidden from us.

All stresses reveal themselves to us as feelings. An ideal state for a human being is (1) a state of balance wherein we feel satisfied, and (2) positive stress, which makes us feel eager to move forward; it is in tandem with our human drives, like hunger, sex drive, and so on.

If stressors are natural or momentary, their effects usually pass once they are catered to. In the example of the woman with the weight problem, if her stressor is malnutrition or hunger, she can just eat something and that stress would disappear. Thereafter, she no longer feels the urge to eat chocolate.

However, if our stressors are not natural or momentary, they must be removed. For example, if the overweight woman's stressor is a lack of self-worth, which is causing her to binge-eat, then she must remove that stressor. Once she successfully gets rid of the stressor, her binge-eating and weight gain will disappear. Once our stressors disappear, our undesirable responses to those stressors disappear too.

Focussing on our Micro-Patterns

As said before, instead of focussing on creating or changing our large patterns directly, we should analyse our smaller patterns first. That will be easier.

Our Environment

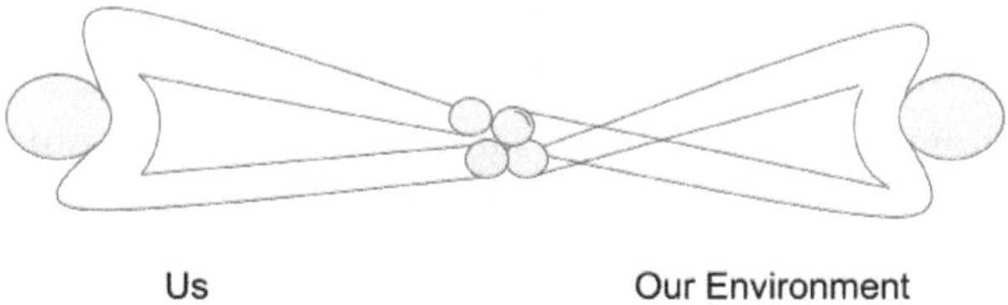

Fig. 7.5: We and our environment are locked together in an embrace, each affecting the other

Our patterns and results are deeply affected by our environment.[25] If the weather is pleasant, we are at ease; if our workplace is conducive to teamwork, we enjoy work; if we have resources, we perform better, and so on. Social psychologists have also noted the surprising power of social networks and how they shape our lives.[26]

---

[25]Gladwell, Malcolm, *Outliers: The Story of Success*, Back Bay Books, 2011.

[26]Christakis, N.A., and J.H. Fowler, *Connected: The Surprising Power of Our*

There are many environmental and psychosocial stressors that affect us and our biorhythms. One such factor is society, which has changed significantly in modern times. Earlier, our society and elders used to guide us when it came to our health, relationships, work, finances, spirituality and even our leisure activities. Today, most of us live in nuclear families.

We must shape our environment such that it becomes an enabler. We must also learn to use the cues in our environment in a positive manner when it comes to triggering our actions.

Our Bodily Senses

Our physical bodies are designed to work in sync with our environment, mind, emotions and actions.

But our body and senses get attuned to stressors to function accordingly. Consider this example: Our ears automatically tune out the noise while working in a chaotic environment.[27] Even the woman with the weight problem, from the example, probably instantly notices a chocolate because her senses are primed to notice it above all things.

Such sense filters, too, are a form of patterns. We can thus change our bodies, too, by consciously examining such patterns.

Social Networks and How They Shape Our Lives, How Your Friends' Friends' Friends Affect Everything You Feel, Think, and Do, Back Bay Books, 2011.

[27]Bregman, A.S., *Auditory Scene Analysis: The Perceptual Organization of Sound*, MIT Press, 1994.

Our Mind

Our mind comprises the following:

- An analytical mind that reasons
- Memory that stores our past experiences
- An ego mind that tells us who we are (or who we desperately want to be)
- A pure intelligence that simply knows

The analytical ability of each mind is different. Some people can instantly grasp numbers and mathematical logic. Others are good at grasping new words. Analytical muscles become stronger with use. For example, taxi drivers in London have highly developed neural connections in a certain part of their brains.[28]

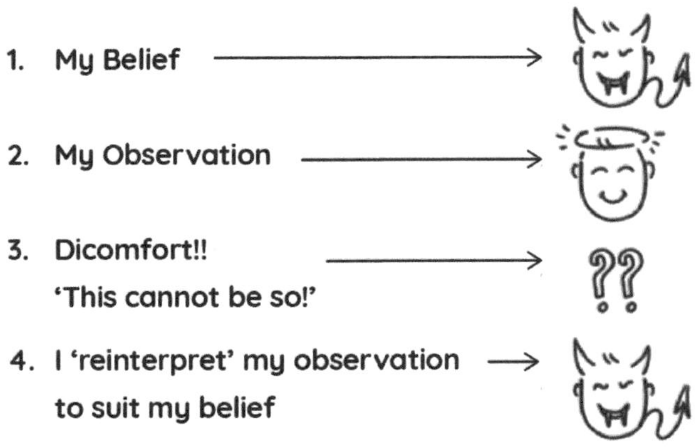

Fig. 7.6: We even distort our perceptions, till they conform to our beliefs.

---

[28]Gladwell, Malcolm, *The Tipping Point: How Little Things Can Make a Big Difference*, Abacus, 2002.

Our memories store past experiences. Some of these are so strong that they become part of beliefs that can totally bypass our analytical brain and distort our current reality. For example, a person who distrusts strangers can choose to interpret the actions of a stranger to conform to their existing belief.

This happens because new things that do not match our past recordings cause us discomfort and stress.

Our ego gives us a sense of self that is separate from others. It gives us our identity, and helps us survive and realize our personal potential. However, our sense of self as a part of others is also crucial. It takes two people to create and nurture us till we grow up. Our environment and society also nurture us.

Our healthy ego allows us to take pride in our achievements and pleasure in interactions with others. But an imbalanced ego can blind us to our own faults and limitations, and make us hypersensitive to the faults of others.

Examining our own ego dispassionately can be difficult. But here is a timeless adage: Truth always cuts the deepest. Therefore, if someone's words or actions hurt us deeply, we may be sure that they have hit at something that we ourselves believe but try very hard to hide from others.

Above all lies our brain's pure, elemental intelligence, which sees everything as it is. Haven't we all felt that powerful, silent inner voice, making us aware that what we are doing is wrong or right?

In the book *Survival of the Sickest*, author Dr Sharon Moalem talks about her late grandfather's urge to donate blood.[29] Her grandfather was forever seeking opportunities to lose blood. He would donate blood, cause himself to bleed, etc.

It turned out that he had hemochromatosis, a disorder that causes iron to build up in one's blood. This can cause an iron overload in one's body, damaging organs like pancreas and liver.

The grandfather's body somehow knew that he needed to lose blood to save itself.

Therefore, we need to know our minds. Otherwise, right now, we could be scripting thousands of our future failures.

Our Emotions

One day, I noticed a wart growing on my right ring finger. It looked ugly, so I just sat down and painstakingly scraped it off.

However, in a couple of days, the wart was back and it was bigger this time. I scraped it off again, and it reappeared again. The same happened at least two or three times till I decided to look for some other solution.

That night I settled myself next to my bedside lamp with a book that I had been waiting to read since long. That lamp had an incandescent bulb that grows very hot in seconds.

I just curled my right finger (where the wart was) and touched the bulb with it. And then I brought back my focus to the book.

---

[29]Moalem, Sharon, Jonathan Prince, *Survival of the Sickest*, Harper Collins, 2007.

> Would you believe it if I told you that after a while, I just forgot about my hurting finger, as I was too absorbed in reading the book? Well, that is how it was. And by the time I removed my finger, a nice big blister had formed on it.
>
> That blister took a few days to heal. But you know what? That wart was gone. And it never reappeared.

I am certainly not advising you to adopt my crazy experiments. This anecdote is only to prove to you that emotions are nothing but powerful resources and they are controllable. Emotions are nothing but the release of certain neurochemicals and neurotransmitters that create our moods and emotional states.

Our analysis gives rise to emotions, which we experience as feelings. If we anticipate danger, we experience fear; if we anticipate something exciting, we feel thrilled; and so on.

However, current or prolonged stressors and intense internal or external inputs can produce prolonged emotional states that deeply affect how we feel and act.

We can understand, control and use our emotions as powerful resources.

Our Actions

Our emotions influence our actions. But it is true that how we act becomes fairly consistent over time. While one person might become aggressive and shout in a situation, another person might turn very quiet and simply withdraw.

As we have seen, stressors exist at the level of our actions too. We must develop skilled actions to support our outcomes.

A Model to Create Patterns

Here is a sequence of steps to help you design suitable patterns for yourself. This technique is called PACE. It stands for:

Fig. 7.7: PACE

- **Picture and plan:** Envision clear goals and create a detailed plan.
- **Awareness:** Develop awareness, analyse and understand your motivations.
- **Craft:** Replace negative patterns with positive ones and build new ones.
- **Evolve:** Employ, reflect and evolve your patterns as needed.

This is so logical that you do not even need to remember it.

The Key to Analysis is Conscious Awareness

Nature has given humans the steering wheel of consciousness to survive in an unpredictable world. We have the ability to 'pattern' ourselves. Our consciousness and our simple patterns, therefore, give us the ability to shape our present and our future.

This is the simple conclusion on which the entire concept of conscious patterns is based.

Fig. 7.8: Consciousness and patterns exist in a continuum

It is important to analyse and know about our patterns and stressors. Given that our past causes most of our stressors, it is important that we start by analysing our past.

Exercise 1 (a): My Past (5–30 Minutes)

> *'Guilt, regret, resentment, grievances, sadness, bitterness, and all forms of non-forgiveness are caused by too much past, and not enough presence.'*
>
> —Eckhart Tolle, *The Power of Now: A Guide to Spiritual Enlightenment*

By understanding your past, you will uncover the causes underlying your present patterns and regain control over them.

This is probably the most important exercise in your life so far. Do it for 10 minutes or 5 hours; it does not matter. The important thing is 'to start'.

Find a restful place. Set an alarm for the time you are

setting aside for the exercise and start. First, relax your body for 2–3 minutes, from the top of your head, going down to the tips of your toes.

Once you feel fully relaxed, let your mind wander back to your earliest memories.

Think of the earliest important events in your life, the various fears, shame, authority figures, triumphs, discoveries and wants.

Then visualize yourself moving forward as a growing child, towards your youth and onwards till your present.

Your rational mind might try to avoid some memories and emotions. Resist this urge because nothing about your past is good, bad or should be seen as a taboo. In fact, your past does not even exist today, except through whatever you hold of it within you.

Once you are done, start writing your life story till date, whatever you can recall of it. Ideally, set aside a notebook for all the written exercises in this book, so that you can refer to it whenever required.

Preferably use a pencil. It helps you correct events as and when you recall them.

Start the process, be it with a single sentence. Resume later, whenever you want.

I would like to share that the first time I sat down to write, I ended up scribbling in 14 pages. That one session taught me more about myself than anything else ever did. I recalled things that I had not consciously thought of in a long time—little incidents, joys, excitements, triumphs, sorrows, stressors, shame and fears. Those memories were inconsequential to others. To me, they must have seemed important enough to have stored them in my memory for so long.

After my first attempt at writing, I realized that the past controls us until we become consciously aware of it and stop it from doing so.

Why must you do this exercise? Because your past exists only in your mind. You must know it but not let it hold you back. You must make it let go of its hold on you and be there only as a useful guide. But to let something go, you must first know that it is holding you back.

Just start writing; you can stop whenever you want.

Now based on your previous exercise, attempt the next one.

Exercise 1 (b): Which patterns of yours really helped you in the past? Which patterns or stressors are holding you back?

(Dear reader, please reproduce the table below in your 'Exercise Notebook' and make notes there.)

Helped me in the past (environment, body, mind, emotions and actions)	*Holding me back (environment, body, mind, emotions and actions)*

Layer III: Design and Deploy Your Patterns with PACE

'If I tell you a story, you can either believe
it or disbelieve it.
Either way, it will get you no closer to the truth.
I am not here to tell you a story.
I am not here to tell you why.
I know the way out of the game, and that
is all that counts.
Never mind why. Let me show you how.'

—Sadhguru, *Adiyogi: The Source of Yoga*

8

The P of PACE: Picture and Plan

'Dare to visualize a world in which your most treasured dreams have become true.'

—Ralph Marston, American writer

To start building patterns, we first need to picture our future and then infer the patterns that we must consciously build, to take us towards that picture.

But first, we must know how to picture our future. People often commit three simple mistakes while doing this. To understand these mistakes, let us revisit our friends Sam and Anita.

It was the last day of their holiday, and Anita and Sam were sitting at the bar, pensive.

'Imagine,' Anita sighed as she toyed with the stem of her glass. 'Tomorrow, we'll be back to the same old routine. I wish we could take more breaks like this. I wish we had a different life.'

'Yes, I know. But...' Sam let the sentence trail away. His shoulders slouched as if in defeat.

'Why can't we just quit our jobs and start something of our own? We have enough saved up. Both of us are experienced. Surely we can think of something!' She made it sound like a question.

'It's not so easy, darling,' Sam replied. 'Look at Vick. He quit a year ago and he's still struggling. Just give me a few more years. Once I make it to the position of VP, it'll all be sorted.'

'Yes,' Anita sniggered. 'Just like when you made it to GM!'

'Now don't start that!'

Anita drained her glass in one gulp and looked away. Sam, too, looked down into his glass, as if seeking answers there. After a while, they paid up and left to catch their flight back to their old life.

Three Common Errors in Picturing our Future

Our first error lies in thinking that our future is far away. We forget that our next moment, too, is our future. Our current moment, too, was the future of the moment that just went by.

An erroneous view makes us miss the significance and urgency of our future goals. We forget that our goals decide the next step we take in the present moment.

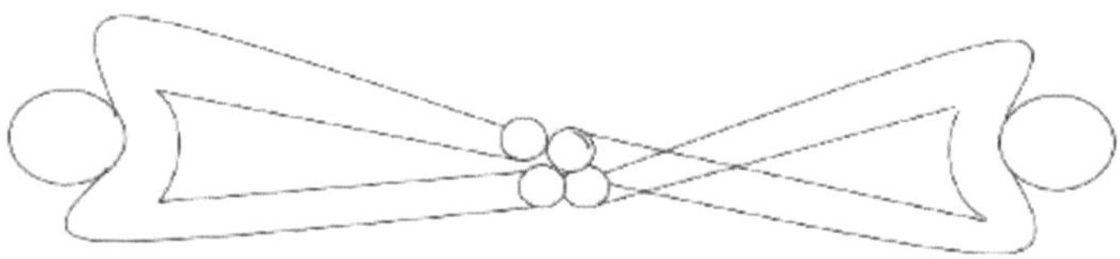

Fig. 8.1: Your future and your present are a continuum

The second common error that we make while planning our future is that we attach ourselves to our expectations from our future.

To picture what our future might be is an important task. But to 'attach' ourselves to our 'expectations' from it is foolishness. It makes us fearful or greedy. We become sorrowful when we do not get what we wanted in the past. Even if we are happy with what we achieved in the past, it is only momentary because we are already fearful or greedy about the next upcoming moment.

When we hold expectations, we also try to speed up or slow down time. When that does not happen, we become frustrated.

'Unease, anxiety, tension, stress, worry—all forms of fear—are caused by too much future, and not enough presence.'

—Eckhart Tolle, author of *The Power of Now: A Guide to Spiritual Enlightenment*

But without holding expectations, how do we still ensure success?

For this, we must understand that our universe might appear to be random, but it is actually probabilistic. As a lay person, this means that when we flip a coin once, the mathematical probability of getting a heads-up is 50 per cent. But if we flip a coin seven times, the probability of getting a heads-up rises to over 99 per cent.

Therefore, if we repeatedly do something, the chances of succeeding at it become higher. We further increase our chances of achieving success by aligning all our patterns towards that outcome.

Accepting an unknown future as something that we cannot control every moment is freedom. This in turn eliminates greed, fear, impatience, frustration and unhappiness from the present moment. It replaces transient highs with an ever-present sense of calm. We become ready for unexpected things and even failure. If we fail, we are then willing to learn from that failure and try again. Isn't this the recipe for happiness? Isn't this also the ideal recipe for success?

> *'In preparing for battle, I have always found that plans are useless but planning is indispensable.'*
>
> —Dwight D. Eisenhower, former US president

When envisioning our future, a common mistake is projecting our present circumstances and anticipating different outcomes. This isn't goal-setting; it's simply prolonging the current reality we seek to alter.

During most of our life as an adult, we mostly aim at work and money as the solutions to every issue. We, however, yearn to enjoy life, to be fit, to dedicate more time to our families, to our higher pursuits, and so on.

Strange, isn't it, that we face west and expect to arrive in the east?

It is true that money is necessary. But if we are not happy with our present even with a lot of wealth, then we will remain unhappy even in the future unless we change our patterns today.

Now that you know what not to do while picturing future goals, perhaps it is time to understand how to decide what the future should be?

How to Set Future Goals

Here are six simple guidelines that you can follow to set future goals:

1. **Understand Maslow's Hierarchy of Needs to rid your vision of fear:** Abraham Maslow, a psychologist, proposed a theory which says that we humans have five sets of needs, all of which follow a hierarchy. Going from the bottom to the top-most level, these needs are physiological, safety and security, love and belonging, esteem and self-actualization. The bottom four needs are deficiency needs, which arise due to deprivation. Once these needs are met, the motivation to cater to these reduces. However, the topmost need—our need for growth—continues to be felt and may even become stronger once we start growing in life. Therefore, visualize yourself in the future, irrespective of where and what you are today, by letting go of the compulsions of security, safety, belongingness, esteem, etc., that drag you away from the higher goal of self-actualization. Focus on how to actualize your capabilities to the fullest. Then build patterns to propel yourself towards that dream.
2. **Set your goal compass:** To achieve self-actualization, align yourself with the passions that excite you, that help you stay in the moment. It does not matter whether your goals related to such passions are grand or small as long as they include what drives you.
3. **Use ikigai:** Once you are able to focus your vision in the right direction, you can use ikigai to make it realizable. Ikigai is the Japanese technique for achieving happiness in life by finding balance between what you love, what you

are good at, what the world needs, and what the world is ready to pay you for.

4. **Balance your goals in all seven dimensions of your life:** You can go after achieving your full potential if no critical area of your life, like health or finances, is pulling you down.
5. **Do a SWOT analysis:** Work on making your goals easier to achieve by doing an analysis of your strengths, weaknesses, opportunities and threats, and aligning your goals with them.
6. **Write down your goals and plans:** Use the power of SMART (specific, measurable, actionable, relevant and time-bound) goals and plans as a template to maintain a list of written goals and plans.

Once your goals are set, you can consciously create patterns to move forward in life. With this understanding, let us move to an exercise to outline the future that you want for yourself.

Exercise 2: Your Vision of Your Future (minimum 10–30 minutes)

Sit comfortably where you will not be disturbed, preferably early in the morning. You can do this for 10 minutes or longer. Just start; you can stop anytime and resume as and when you like.

Close your eyes and for 2–3 minutes, relax your body from head to toe.

Once fully relaxed, allow your mind to see you as you are in your future, not as an image, but vividly, like in a movie, with all details. Perhaps you are in your favourite car, driving where you want to, with someone you love, doing what excites you.

Do not worry about how you got there. Do not imagine any constraints. You do not have to prove anything to anyone. This is about creating what you want. Your dreams are unique. You do not want to reach the end of your life filled with regret, realizing that you have lived catering to someone else's dreams.

If you are not able to envision yourself or your future, then maybe you are yet to discover where or what you want to be, or maybe you still have to work on believing that you can get there. Even if this is so, do not worry. Like everything else, clarity about your goals is a muscle pattern. It develops with constant repetition.

After completing this exercise, list whatever you visualized for yourself and whatever future patterns you saw in and around yourself. Draw a diagram, list points, write a note, or use a combination of these methods. Do whatever works for you.

You can categorize whatever you visualized as your goals, and list all of it down as per the major areas of your life:

- Self
    - Body
    - Mind
    - Emotions
    - Actions
- Financial Health
- Work
- Relationships
- Leisure
- Giving (to others and to your environment)
- Spiritual pursuits

Feel free to add to or change these categories.

Personally, I like to list down the big picture or my broader goals under each category when I visualize my future.

Look at the sample in the first column of the table given below. It is an abridged version of my own vision and the patterns that I found were important in order to create the life I had envisioned. Create your own vision list and refine it as your clarity grows. A vision, however, does not show you the steps that you must take to get there. These steps are the patterns that you must create. Samples of such patterns are listed in the second column of the table below.

Table. 8.1

A Sample Vision and the Patterns Needed

Vision (This is written in present tense because this is how visioning works. You visualize and 'feel' your future as if it were happening to you in the present moment.)	**Patterns** (These, too, are listed in the present tense for the same reason.)
Overall • I am limitless. • I live in this beautiful, small, quiet place, with a lawn in the front of my house and trees in the courtyard. • My wife and I travel a lot to meet our children and friends.	• Making family and friends priority • Travelling • Inspiring and fun professional life • Operational independence of my companies and teams

• I write, and travel for my business meetings, book launches, signings, etc. • I only pick up work that inspires me. • My companies are operationally independent and are massively impacting the lives of millions of people.	
Body health • I am fit and weigh 68 kg. • I am flexible. • I am internally healthy.	• Following fit and healthy lifestyle in general • Doing regular movements and being mindful of correct postures • Doing regular stretches • Performing eight *suryanamaskar*s and breathing exercises each morning under the sun • Cycling • Drinking water first thing every morning, the last thing every night, and always carrying a bottle of water
Mind • My mind is calm, organized, logical, attentive and curious. • My memory is sharp.	• Meditating at least on the weekends • Focussing on one thing at a time • Writing in my journal

Emotions • My emotions help me create the motives that I need to act. • I control my emotions, not the other way around.	• Not letting emotions bypass analytical brain • Analysing what gives rise to certain emotions and finding methods that help me generate the emotions needed
Energy • I am energetic.	• Remove all energy blockers and work on energy boosters, like breathing, good postures and a healthy diet • Stay away from people who sap positive energy
Finances and business • I am financially free. • My business has 'x' assets. • I am running my business like a well-oiled engine.	• Having a financial consultant who handles finances • Investing a certain amount each month • Keeping channels through which money keeps trickling in • Having a well-thought-out business model • Having efficient employees • Having a wide customer base • Training and upskilling employees and self

Relationships • I enjoy excellent relationships with my family and friends.	• Being responsive • Always keeping promises
Leisure • I travel, read and write. • I also play a musical instrument.	• Planning leisure activities in the same detailed manner in which I plan my work • Choosing an instrument and practising how to play on it
Spirituality • I believe in the principle of oneness and gratitude.	• Practising gratitude each day

To inch closer to your vision, break your vision into steps. These patterns or steps, which you will list in the second column of the table, must be clear, such that you can break them into smaller steps if needed.

If these steps are abstractions, you will not know when and how to take the next step. If the steps are not broken down well, they might appear complex. Once you break these large steps into smaller, specific, measurable ones, you can practise them on a day-to-day or moment-to-moment basis. These will then become internal patterns.

For example, if you want to write a book, you need to understand that a book is a compilation of chapters in a certain sequence, which are further compilations of sections, paragraphs, sentences and words. Your book will materialize only when you cater to all individual elements.

Then there are external patterns. You can surround yourself with others' writings to inspire yourself, read reference material, talk to authors who can guide you, take the help of people and tools to edit and publish what you write, and so on. All of this will help you write your book.

Zig Ziglar, famous American author and motivational speaker, said, 'For ten or fifteen years, I was "going to" write a book. You know anybody who's "gonna" do just a whole lot of things, folks? I was going to write a book. But it wasn't until I got busy, writing the book, and writing the plans first, before the book ever materialized.'[30]

You too need to do the same—start defining a vision. Then break it down consciously into the little patterns that will take you towards that vision.

After writing your vision in the first column, break it down into smaller steps in the second column. Just write what you can figure out at this moment. Once you start learning how to become aware of your patterns, come back and add to the column. It is a cyclic process.

Below is a method that I have evolved over the years. This involves summarizing my vision and goals in seven sheets:

- Sheet 1: Entire life
- Sheet 2: The next five years
- Sheet 3: The current year, preferably broken into quarters
- Sheet 4: The current month, broken down into weeks
- Sheet 5: The current week
- Sheet 6: Tomorrow
- Sheet 7: Today. This is a little post-it or a Google Keep note for the day

[30]'Zig Ziglar Setting Goals 1 of 3', YouTube, 2 November 2007, https://tinyurl.com/3c4pn8wt. Accessed on 13 March 2024.

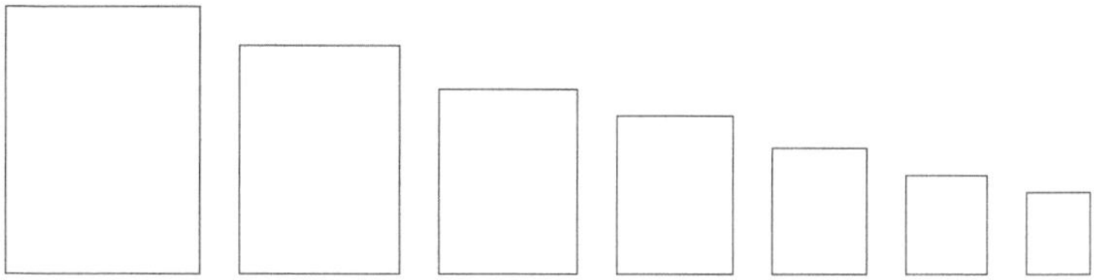

Fig. 9.2: A plan for life

You can maintain the first three, that is, the long-term sheets in a folder or save their soft copies. The rest you may record in any form you wish to. This will free you from the daily struggle of trying to figure out your long- or short-term goals. Everything stays in one place. If needed, you can revise what you must do on a particular day or the next, or maybe during the week or month. For long-term changes, you can update the other sheets annually or update them whenever you wish to.

While writing on these sheets, your mind might get flooded with thoughts like, 'Should I be doing this or that? What should I focus on now? What is superfluous and must be dropped if it does not add value to my life tomorrow and today?'

Doing this exercise can be empowering. It will give you the clarity to say 'no' to almost anything that is not in line with your goal compass. It will help declutter your mind.

The resulting clarity will leave you feeling relaxed, creative, clear, fully in the present—not swayed by FOMO (fear of missing out) or tantalizing shortcuts that lead you on wild goose chases, but aware and fulfilled with what you are doing right now.

Whenever a thought arises, you can examine it in the context of the larger picture.

9

The A of PACE: Awareness

'Truth has no path. Truth is living and, therefore, changing. Awareness is without choice, without demand, without anxiety; in that state of mind, there is perception. To know oneself is to study oneself in action with another person. Awareness has no frontier; it is giving of your whole being, without exclusion.'

—Bruce Lee, martial artist

The second step in creating patterns is to become aware of our current self and of the patterns within and around us.

Awareness underlies everything, be it in our deepest sleep, a state of coma, or amidst our greatest distractions. It is perhaps our fundamental intelligence. It manages our self.

Awareness = Truth (Observation + Knowledge + Acceptance of That Knowledge)

Awareness is truth. So, the first step to know who we truly are is to stop lying to our own self. If we lie to ourself, we soon start to lose all understanding of who we are along with the knowledge of everything around us.

Knowledge might also require analysis. For example, we might find it difficult to understand why we get angry. The emotion in question should be broken down and analysed. This will lead us to the root cause. Knowing the causes is nothing but knowledge.

And awareness is also the acceptance of knowledge and the acceptance of truth. However, in today's time, our awareness has become a commodity that everyone is trying to capture. All our senses are bombarded by various electronic media. Our awareness gets deluged under their assault and our fundamental intelligence drowns. Even simple things start to appear complex. Life itself turns into a mystery and we start losing control over ourselves.

Therefore, it is not surprising that everyone is struggling to understand happiness, relationships, money, work, leisure, survival, and other such cornerstones of human life. We can know who we are and how to get where we want to go only when we manage to regain control of our awareness.

After returning from that fateful trip, Anita and Sam continued to think about their future.

Within a few days of their return, they both sat down and had a serious conversation. After that conversation, they visualized their goals and what they wanted their present to be. Then, they wrote down their vision and jotted down the patterns they would have to follow in order to attain the envisioned goals.

They gained a better understanding of the fact that there was a mismatch between where they wanted to be and where they were.

They now started to consciously think about and analyse their present circumstances.

Awareness involves:

- Awareness of environment
- Awareness of self

It also involves analysing and getting to the roots of our stressors, both within ourselves and in our environment. Let us start with our environment.

Awareness of Environment

In his book *The Tipping Point*, Malcolm Gladwell shows us that the environment has a powerful impact on us. He takes the example of a TV advertising study that concluded, 'Television advertisements would be more effective if the visual display created repeated vertical movements of the television viewers' heads.'[31]

The study showed that a TV advertisement can make us buy a product just by causing us to move our head up and down, while watching the advertisement. It does not matter whether the advertisement makes us 'nod' our head in agreement to something said in it or it does so by showing us a ball bouncing up and down in the advertisement. In both cases, we become more likely to buy that product just by 'nodding' our head.

Doesn't that sound shocking? It shows us that something 'outside' of us can make us react, often without us even realizing it. But this also gives us a wonderful opportunity, as it means that by understanding and shaping things outside

[31]Gladwell, Malcolm, *The Tipping Point: How Little Things Can Make a Big Difference*, Little, Brown and Company, 2000.

of us—our environment—we too can influence our reactions in the way we desire. This can be done by considering some of the following points:

- To organize our surroundings, we should first organize ourselves.
- We should surround ourself with resources, more knowledge, etc., to become wiser, more productive, and so on. Top organizations and universities follow this.
- We should watch, listen to and expose ourselves to happy things. In a study conducted to test whether emotions are contagious in computer-mediated communication (like social media communications), the researchers concluded that 'emotional contagion took place'. This means that negative people can infect others with their negative emotions.[32] Similarly, charismatic people infect others with their emotions. So, we should hang out with charismatic people, modify our inner circle, work on our relationship with the people in our areas of influence and interest, as it will help us become what we want to be.[33]

Everything in our environment is either patterns or chaos. Even the chaos we see has patterns underneath that are yet to be figured out. So, by understanding our environment,

---

[32]Hancock, Jeffrey, et al., 'I'm Sad You're Sad', Department of Communication, Cornell University, 2008, https://tinyurl.com/4ax74pe2. Accessed on 20 May 2024.

[33]According to the evolutionary psychologist, Robin Dunbar, people are cognitively able to maintain only a certain number of stable relationships at once. This number is known as 'Dunbar's number'. The number proposed by him was 150.

reshaping it when we can, aligning ourselves to it when we cannot, and preparing our conscious self to deal with all that is unpredictable, we can change our life at the most complex levels by shaping it at its most fundamental levels, like the way we sit, walk, talk, eat, manage work, relationships, finances, and so on.

Awareness of Self

We have been taught to look outwards for wisdom, but most of us have lost connection with the immense knowledge that lies within us. To regain this fundamental awareness, we need to be aware of the four fundamental levels at which our self exists: the biological body, mind, emotions and actions.[34]

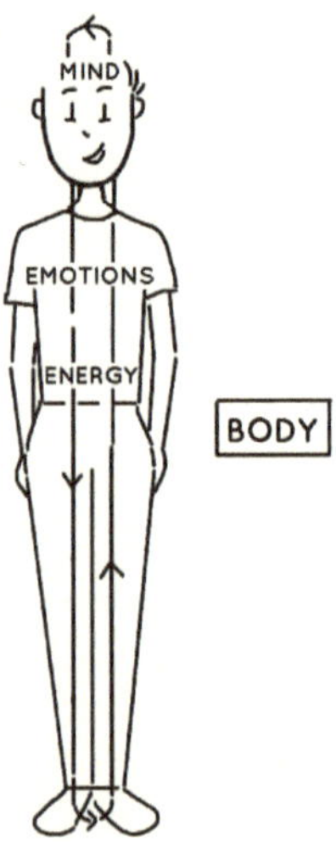

Fig. 9.1: Our self comprises our body, mind, emotions and actions

---

[34]Sadhguru and Arundhathi Subramaniam, *Adiyogi: The Source of Yoga*, HarperCollins, India, 2017, p. 128–9.

These four aspects of our self are shaped by:

- Our past
- Our present
- Our future

We have already learnt about past patterns earlier in the book and about future plans in the previous chapter. Now, let us look at what comprises our present self.

Our Body

In my software development firm, 20-year-olds hunch over their bright laptop screens with intense concentration, elbows on workstations, necks and backs curved, rarely blinking. Only their fingers move. They wear thick glasses. The older ones suffer from dry eyes, nausea, spondylitis, backache, numb fingers, and so on. Warn them and they usually say, 'I know, but...'

Here is some advice in this regard by one of the greatest entrepreneurs of his time.

Narayan Murthy, the founder of Infosys, one of India's largest software services firms, reportedly told a co-passenger during a flight, 'Sometimes my knee hurts, I should have taken better care of my body. When I was young I was so busy working that I never got time to take care of myself, and now even if I want to work more, I can't. My body doesn't permit it.'

He went on, 'You are young. You are smart and ambitious but don't repeat the mistake I made. Take proper care of your body and take proper rest. This is the only body you have got.'

The effect of everything that we do is communicated to us by our body. Therefore, the patterns of our bodies affect every single outcome of ours.

Even a basic level of awareness of your body will make you aware of your body patterns. Are your spine and neck erect or curved? Are your knees strong or do you have trouble squatting and getting back up? Do you always sit on a chair or on the floor sometimes? Is your back always supported against something or propped up by your elbows? Is your pulse fast, slow, uneven or rhythmic? Are your nose and lungs generally clear or clogged? Do you breathe rhythmically or unevenly? Are you a smiler, brooder or frowner? Do you have the perfect vision? Are your nails pale, yellowing or pink; chipped, ridged or smooth; convex, flat or concave? Is your tongue coated? Are your teeth and gums strong, chipped or gone?

How do you feel inside? What do you generally eat or drink? Do you feel bloated or starved or satiated? Does your body process junk well or does that make you miserable? Is your sex drive low, normal or excessive?

What kind of activities is your body best suited for? Is it suited for the outdoors or indoors? Are you tall or short, sporty or academic?

I can go on and on, but I am sure you get the point now.

With awareness, we begin to discover and question how and why we are who we are. We come to realize the massive effects of our environment on our body. For example, a majority of us sit on a chair most of the time, so that our backs are usually supported by the backrest of the chair or by our elbows on a table. But we still wonder why our back is weak, why it aches or sprains easily, or why we tire easily. We wonder why we cannot squat or get back up, why our legs, knees and ankles begin to give up, become unstable, why we stumble or fall easily as we grow old. We usually take our bodies, minds, emotions, actions and our surrounding patterns for granted.

This was a tiny example. If we keep looking and analysing, our lives will change. The very first time I did so, I realized the reasons behind feeling fatigued—not blinking enough, not taking care of my eyes, not keeping my nose clear, not having enough water, not chewing food long enough, and ignoring natural biorhythms just to get more work done.

Our Mind

Our mind is also a tool. It creates our sense of self (ego); stores information (memory); applies logic and generates options (analytical brain); and holds a deep intelligence (our fundamental intelligence).

The mind, like any tool, can be studied, understood and controlled, and that is best done by our own self.

Is your mind organized, knowledgeable, clear, calm and controlled, or is it disorganized, unskilled, untrained, confused, wandering, hyperactive, impulsive and paralysed with fear of the unknown?

Are your memories helpful experiences of the past, making you open and observant, reflective and analytical, or are they debilitating beliefs that keep you stuck within yourself and force you to become judgemental?

Are you aware of your self-image? Is that self-image who you really are or is it merely a projection? Is your ego comfortable with itself and others, appreciative and expansive, or uncomfortable, envious, critical and small-minded?

Is your mind in line with what and where you wish to be, right now and later?

You will realize that your mind is totally controllable if you look for and target its roots. A friend was writing his first book but could not proceed beyond the start, as he kept obsessing about how others would judge the book. A simple piece of advice—asking him to write only for himself—removed that block and he had the book completed in no time.

The beauty lies in the fact that once we begin to see patterns, we cannot unsee them.

Our environment affects our mental patterns, too. If our surroundings support reflection, we are more likely to be reflective. If our colleagues are knowledgeable, our knowledge grows. If we begin to organize our surroundings and ourselves, including our minds, our memory capacity and recall speed start increasing instantly and dramatically.

Our Emotions

Emotions are chemical rushes that drive us to do something. Both love and rage can cause people to do things that might otherwise seem impossible. Suffering and bliss change our entire personality. Without emotions to drive us, we would not be able to act.

Emotions are caused by thoughts and vice versa. Many emotions are triggered by our past experiences, too. These emotions are automatic, unthinking and completely patterned.

If we think of emotions as abstractions, they appear difficult to understand. But we can interpret our emotions by analysing our thoughts and actions as being under the influence of emotions. Why did we fly into a rage at such and such a time? What were our senses focussed upon in the moment? What triggered us? Was the trigger internal or external? What were we thinking of or were we not thinking at all? What was our underlying emotion? Can we bring about that same emotion at will? What would it take? What is our default emotion when we are doing nothing?

Once again, we might find that many of the underlying causes are simple. I found myself pessimistic on Tuesdays due to overloading myself on Mondays (and ending up with a huge workload on Tuesdays). My impulsiveness and impatience turned out to be acquired patterns from my days in the army—from having to take quick, sometimes life-and-death decisions, and from demanding immediate actions. Most of the times, both emotions turned out to be irrelevant to me in my life outside the army.

Our emotions are not us. They must serve us. We can create, control and channelize our emotions by controlling our environment and triggers. We can generate happiness and contentment at will and use these to move towards our goals. Therefore, our emotions and feelings, too, are resources for us.

Our Actions

Our actions are the observable expressions of our energy. They are like the movement of a car's wheels. Hundreds of things happen in a car to make those wheels move. At last, it is this movement that makes a car useful. If the wheels do not move, then everything else in a car is meaningless.

Actions can be observed. So, they act as clues to understanding the rest that is not observable. And, once we understand how actions happen, we can understand the patterns of our actions and we can shape those patterns to shape the rest of us.

As we saw earlier, even our complex action patterns can be broken down into smaller parts till they become understandable and controllable. For example, the book *Total Immersion: The Revolutionary Way To Swim Better, Faster, and Easier* by Terry Laughlin and John Delves teaches you swimming by breaking down the seemingly complex act of swimming into basic movements and patterns, making it extremely simple to learn.

How Do We Even Know That We Are Aware?

We know that we are aware when:

- We begin to perceive the tiny patterns that are influencing us.
- We become aware of our body, mind, emotions, actions and our environment at the basic level.
- Our awareness persists even when we are exhibiting unconscious behaviours, thus enabling us to discern when our unconscious self begins to take control.

Exercise 3: Awareness of Present Self and Environment

'All negativity is caused by an accumulation of psychological time and denial of the present.'

—Eckhart Tolle, author of *The Power of Now: A Guide to Spiritual Enlightenment*

Exercise 1 helped you unravel your past patterns and Exercise 2 made you define the patterns that you need to create. This exercise will help you identify your current patterns—within and outside—so that you can identify those that you must modify. It starts with three questions to help you identify some of your key patterns. Answer these questions in your exercise notebook. Make sure to do this exercise, even if it is for just a minute.

Exercise 3 (a): What are your small or large successes and failures in life? Why did you succeed or fail? What were the underlying patterns that drove your successes and failures—internal or external? Ask 'why'. Do it five times, or as many times as needed, to get to the root patterns or causes.

Exercise 3 (b): What do you get most complimented for and why? What are the most common things you get checked for, and what are the reasons behind them? Use these whys to again lead you to the underlying patterns.

Exercise 3 (c): What are the things that you have to be dragged away from, the things that make you forget time (your interests)? Why is this so? What things make you procrastinate (things that do not interest you) and why? Answers to these questions will lead you to your underlying nature, your unique likes and dislikes. These are patterns that come naturally to you. Also, ask why is that so. In case you wish to change such a pattern, you could do so by changing the underlying 'why'.

A friend of mine loved playing computer games, gambling at the casino, watching movies, reading or learning something new, writing, and so on. However, doing all of these activities consumed and drained him eventually. The underlying causes turned out to be his love for challenges and adding fuel to fire his imagination. Realizing the limited time at his disposal, he dropped computer games, the casino, etc., and instead focussed on watching movies, reading and writing, all of which interested him equally and also benefitted him more.

Exercise 3 (d): With the insights gained from the answers to the previous three questions, examine your current self and your environment. Again, this could be an ongoing exercise, one you can pause at any moment. But you must start! Do this for at least 10 minutes, then pick it up later, thus making it a work in progress.

Sit anywhere with your notebook and a pencil. Pay attention to yourself for 2–3 minutes. Begin to examine yourself, your environment, body, mind, emotions and energy.

Look at the sample table provided at the end of this chapter. Use the categories mentioned in the sample table or create your own. Do whatever suits you best.

Then start listing your current patterns.

Try to analyse each pattern by repeatedly asking, 'Why?' Some of these patterns might be basic ones that you could directly apply, modify or drop. Others might look complex, but your whys will lead you to simple yet powerful hidden root patterns. Those are the ones that you should work on controlling.

Be as specific as you can; you will then be able to be equally specific while reshaping your patterns.

Here are some examples for Exercise 3 (d):

- I procrastinate by pushing things for later by saying, 'After five minutes!' I do this because I avoid tasks and decisions that seem unpleasant. They make me feel uncomfortable. They call upon knowledge or capabilities that I feel I do not have. Stepping beyond my current capabilities makes me uncomfortable and fearful. I fear I will fail and invite ridicule. Inside me, I hide a feeling of inadequacy and self-ridicule. I lack acceptance and esteem for myself. I felt treated as a lesser person by my elders when I was young. (Now, this constant sense of inadequacy, of not being good enough, or assuming you lack knowledge are patterns that need to be eradicated. You will find that your habit of procrastinating, too, gets eradicated as you become capable of listening to criticism without feeling put down, and begin to take decisions without hesitation or fear of failure or ridicule.)

- I get angry when faced with disagreements. Others' words threaten to expose what I feel are my hidden weaknesses. I need external assurances to prove my worth. My own self-worth and internal affirmations are not enough. (So, you can see that the root cause of this pattern, too, is a sense of inadequacy, which is what you must eradicate to ultimately not get angry, or sarcastic, when faced with disagreements.)
- I avoid thinking big and subconsciously avoid big opportunities because I am not used to them. I feel incapable of taking them on. I fear failure. Why? Because I crave external approval. I lack an inner sense of self-approval. This is so because I was rarely appreciated as a child. (Such a realization will help the person start to develop self-worth and start thinking big. This positive cycle replaces the earlier negative one.)
- I am low on energy. This is because I do not drink enough water and I do not eat right. (If this is so, simply start drinking enough water and start eating right, and your lethargy will vanish.)

This exercise is amazing. You will find that many of your patterns arise from the same roots. These roots are far fewer. Once you change these few root patterns, you will see changes in a huge number of your branches and fruits, too.

How Awareness of the Self Helps in Crafting Patterns

You can decide which current patterns you must strengthen, which ones you must shed or reshape, and which new ones you must craft. While deciding this, come up with patterns that suit your unique self. Do not blindly copy patterns that others follow. Each person's unique self dictates what patterns work for them. Here is an example of two persons, with different personalities, wanting to lose weight.

80-Year-Old Man	**35-Year-Old Woman**
• An intelligent and lonely old man who leads a sedentary life. • He is disorganized, unplanned and impulsive.	• An intelligent woman, who stays with her husband, is self-employed and has many friends. • She is highly organized, planned and disciplined.
• He feels unloved and is afraid of dying alone. • He is weak-willed and has low motivation to lose weight. ('Nobody cares for me anyway. Does it even matter?') • He is cynical and unbelieving. • He is also a little miserly and hates to spend.	• She is carefree and confident. • She is strong-willed. ('I must lose weight! I only need to know how.') • She is trusting and likes to follow advice. • She does not mind spending money for a good reason.

• The root causes behind him gaining weight are drinking and comfort snacking. He has liquor and snacks lying around at home and gravitates to them to pass his time.	• The root cause behind her gaining weight is her love for soft drink. She finds them fun and has these a little too often, but she has failed to link this to her weight gain. Her cue for drinking a cola is finding one lying around in her refrigerator or whenever her friends drop in.

The patterns that might help these two lose weight are quite different. Their possible solutions are as follows:

80-Year-Old Man	**35-Year-Old Woman**
• He can be in the company of someone who cares. • He can increase his social activity. • He can surround himself with friends and family.	• She can hire a fitness trainer or coach for online or offline sessions to help her lose weight. • She can work on gaining knowledge about why she is putting on weight.

Exercise 3 (e): Your Current Patterns

This is a sample of recurring patterns that people often wish to do something about. It is summarized from interactions with trainees in my patterns workshops.

Current Patterns	Whys (This will help take you to the root cause[s])
Body	
'I weigh 110 kg. I am unfit. My body is inflexible.'	• I do not exercise regularly and instead go on yo-yo diets. • I do not find the time to exercise. • I take on too much, maybe to prove to others that I am worthy. • I often feel that I am not worthy.
'My eyes tire quickly and cause an overall sense of fatigue. I frown subconsciously while reading or focussing on anything.'	• I do not exercise my eyes. • I work for long stretches, without taking breaks in between to rest my eyes.
'I often get physically exhausted.'	• I am dehydrated. • I have irregular eating habits. • I do not chew my food properly. • I have poor sitting posture.
'My digestion is poor.'	• I might have a fatty liver and would need to get it checked.
Mind	
'I'm imaginative and full of ideas.'	• I am fond of reading. • I have strong visualization. • I daydream.

'My mind wanders.'	• I've never tried to control and organize my mind. • There is always too much going on in my mind. • I take on too many tasks. • I do not say no to things. • I do not prioritize and feel okay with letting go of a few things.
'I am not able to retain much information about people.'	• I do not pay attention to people. • My interest in people is low. • I am not an extrovert. • I focus on my responses while interacting.
Emotions	
'When things go wrong, I blame others.'	• I try to hide my own mistakes. • I hate accepting my own mistakes. • I feel that others will laugh at me if they think I am wrong. • I hate being laughed at because as the younger sibling, I got laughed at often.
'I lose my temper.' 'I am resentful.'	• I interpret disagreements as criticism. • I take criticism as a finger pointing at me, saying, 'You are not good enough.'
'I envy people with more wealth.' 'I compete.'	• I feel money will bring me recognition and power. • I feel inadequate and 'small' without external validation and that is my default state.
'I am usually happy and pleasant.'	• I have limited needs. • It is an acquired pattern.

Action Patterns and Energy	
'Parties drain me; conferences exhaust me; if too many people are around me, I cannot focus.'	• I am trying too hard to be too many things to too many people, and thus end up exhausting my energy. • Disagreeing with them might cause unpleasantness, and I hate unpleasantness. • I back down in front of pushy people, just as I used to do as a child.
'Time spent with my family energizes me.'	• I am carefree around my family. • I can be who I am with them, and do not have to keep up any pretence. • I keep up pretences when with others.
'I cannot do anything else while a deadline is looming. Deadlines make my mind buzz and choke my energy.'	• I attach too much significance to deadlines and invest too much of myself. • I withdraw from everything else for that duration. • I hate failure; I feel that my failures reflect upon me. • My self-image is weak. Thus, I give too much significance to what others think or say about me.
'I carry the energy of passivity—I react rather than act.' 'I take things as not being in my control.' 'I get tired easily.'	• I lack confidence. • I fear failure.

'I lack these certain skills.'	• I find it difficult to focus on them. • I do not analyse them well or work upon the micro-skills that underlie them.
Money and Finances	
'I have no major liabilities.'	• I have limited needs. • I do not feel the need to hoard. • I am satisfied with myself and the way I am.
'My finances are disorganized.'	• I never spent time on organizing them. • I never realized the importance of organizing my finances earlier.
'I hoard money.'	• I feel money gives me power, and I love power. • I think that without money, I will have little power, and no one will listen to me.
'I waste money.'	• I show off. • I want to keep up with the Joneses. • I feel inadequate.
'I have few investments.'	• I barely invest. • I lack the prerequisite knowledge.
Work and Business	
'My employees are not close to me.'	• I do not invest time with them. • I do not have any prior experience in handling a business.
'I get bogged down with things at the operational level.'	• I have a controlling mindset. • I do not delegate or appreciate others' work.

'I have no work–life balance.'	• My work is disorganized. • My work processes are not in place. • I am a perfectionist. • I try to do everything myself. • I like to be 'the fire fighter' and like to be appreciated.
'I am good at selling. My company is strong in sales.'	• I practise my selling skills. • I train my sales team regularly. • I enjoy selling. • I am persistent. • I can take a 'no' and go on.
'My business is poor at marketing.'	• I lack the knowledge and experience needed for marketing. • I do not understand digital marketing. • No one in my company understands digital marketing.
'I take too long to complete my work.'	• I am a slow reader. • I type too slowly.
Relationships	
'My relationships are not great.'	• I hold unrealistic expectations. • I am insecure. • I need constant reassurance. • I don't feel loved for who I am.
'I am unreliable.'	• I do not keep my promises. • I am always too busy. • I take on too much in an effort to prove myself. • I feel I am not good enough.
'I cannot hold a friendship for long.'	• I am poor at following up. • I am bad at time management.

10

The C of PACE: Craft Your Patterns

'Measure a thousand times and cut once.'

—Turkish proverb

You have now reached the heart of the patterns game—consciously crafting your patterns. Crafting patterns can be broken down further into a four-step process called BERT.

BERT stands for:

- **Blueprint the right patterns:** You create the right patterns to serve you.
- **Enable:** Surround yourself with enablers, inside and outside.
- **Rhythmize:** Rhythmize your patterns, so that they can be repeated without a lot of effort.
- **Tinker:** Tinker with your patterns whenever and wherever required.

Fig. 10.1: Blueprint 'rhythms' within and around you

The ultimate aim is to get your patterns to work effortlessly for you, so that your self is conscious and free to notice the new possibilities around you.

11

BERT 1: Blueprint the Right Patterns

'Whatever you decide to do, make sure it makes you happy.'

—Paulo Coelho, novelist

Now that we've identified the patterns we want to create, let us start creating them.

A blueprint commonly refers to a detailed plan or design in which we lay down the specifications, dimensions and features of a structure or object before it is constructed or implemented. Just as we need a well-crafted blueprint to make a good building, we need a good blueprint to build a pattern that we can use repeatedly. If the blueprint of a building is flawed, the building can fall. Similarly, if the blueprint of a pattern is flawed, the said pattern will lead to failure. Conversely, a sound blueprint will create a powerful pattern.

To create the right blueprint for a pattern, ensure that these four things are right:

- **Right roots:** This means focussing on the simple root patterns or causes, not on abstract effects.
- **Right methods:** This means adopting methods that actually lead to results. Often, people pick up methods that are ineffective or even harmful.
- **'Right for you' patterns:** This means adopting methods that fit your unique personality, that are enjoyable and also easy for you.
- **Right techniques:** Suppose running suits you. In that case, ensure you use the correct form and technique of running to maximize benefits and prevent discomfort while running.

Right Roots

As the first step, you must change the stressors, beliefs and root patterns that give rise to your complex big blockers. False ego-state(s) like 'I'm not okay, you're okay' hold you back.

Don't focus on your past experiences, as they will negatively impact many of your outcomes in the future. Focus on your default emotions and correct them. Along with that, focus on your environment and analyse the resources you can use.

Changing higher patterns will be superficial without removing the stressors. For example, unless the woman who cannot stop herself from eating chocolate finds relief from the underlying stress that causes her to eat chocolate, she will continue to be like a primed bomb, waiting for a trigger to set off her cravings.

Focus on your actions as well, as they too affect sensations, thoughts, emotions and environment. A well-known study supporting this hypothesis was conducted by German social psychologist Fritz Strack and his colleagues in 1988.[35] In this study, the psychologists selected a set of volunteers who would watch an animated movie. They found something astounding. Volunteers who watched the movie with pens clenched between their teeth—which forced them to smile—found the movie much funnier! Others who watched the movie with pens held between inward-folded lips—that prevented them from smiling and made them frown instead—found the movie less funny in comparison!

Therefore, actions do not just reflect our emotions, they also team up to create them. If you tell yourself that you are awesome, smile and use words that reflect that you are happy—you will eventually end up feeling happy. In other words, 'Fake it till you make it!'

The good news is that most of these root patterns are very simple to adopt. Even those root patterns that are long-standing internal or environmental states are changeable. For example, internal states like 'I'm not good enough!' are not our natural state of being. A baby is not born feeling that way. Our external experiences lead to the creation of such states. A person grows up watching their parents fight (experience) and concludes (interprets) that relationships cause conflicts (belief). Thereafter, they avoid relationships (behaviour).

Experience > Interpretation > Pattern of Belief
(or State) > Behaviour(s)

---

[35]Strack, Fritz, Leonard Martin and S. Stepper, 'Inhibiting and Facilitating Conditions of the Human Smile: A Nonobtrusive Test of the Facial Feedback Hypothesis', *Journal of Personality and Social Psychology*, Vol. 54, 1988, pp. 768–77.

Once you understand your internal states, most of these will lose their grip on you. Go the whole hog. Change the vocabulary or lexicon or root patterns of your body, mind, emotions, energy and environment. Do this for all that matters to you. Whatever enterprise you choose in life, make sure to understand its patterns. You only need to be aware and analyse. Get to the roots and shape them.

Right Methods

The year was 1989, five years after I joined the Indian Army. It was also the year that I married Archana. Life was going really well. But within nine years of first getting into army life as a cadet, I injured my knees severely and, possibly, permanently. The reason was extreme exercise, and that too without guidance. From a lifestyle of little physical activity, within a short period, I had moved to a life of extreme physical exertion. My tiny but repeated incorrect patterns of physical exercise chipped away, slowly but surely, at my knees. It did not help that I had also been slightly bow-legged since birth. That probably added to the injury in my knees.

Doctors found that the discs in both my knees had worn out and the bones in these joints were grating against one another—this was excruciatingly painful. I was told that an operation would relieve the pain, but I would not be able to run thereafter. That was not an option for me. I had many years of army life ahead of me.

So, I let things go on as they were. Whenever it was time to participate in any exercise involving running, I would go ahead with it, hiding my pain as best as I could, and hobbling for days after. It was painful but unavoidable.

A decade passed. Then, in 1999, my regiment was ordered to move to a new theatre of operations. I was appointed to lead an advance party; 100-odd soldiers were tasked with moving ahead and preparing things before the rest of the regiment arrived. Shivi, a young subaltern, accompanied me as my second-in-command.

It wasn't long before my subaltern friend noticed the condition of my knees. He was extremely fit and exercised daily. I did not join him, as I did not want to injure my knees further. Taking note, he suggested that I try some sitting postures.

What the heck, I thought. I did not believe that corrective sitting postures or static exercises of any kind could help me. But as I did not have anything to lose, I joined him.

All he did was teach me a couple of sitting postures. It did seem to provide some relief, so I started practising those regularly. Soon, I adopted those postures as my regular sitting patterns (creating patterns consciously was already second nature to me). Soon, I began to sit that way, without even noticing it. Those postures became subconscious patterns.

Before this, I had already taken to sticking nails in the outer edges of the soles of my shoes to stop myself from walking bow-legged.

A few months later, when the time for a routine cross-country run came around, both my subaltern and I ran. Knowing my condition, he offered to pace me.

When that run began, I was anticipating the pain in my knees to kick in like always.

What followed was astonishing. Halfway through the run, my subaltern said, 'Sir, I cannot keep up with you any longer. Please go on!'

I ran that entire distance without a twinge in either of my knees. The pain in my knees had totally vanished! To rule out that this might be a fluke, I ran longer distances many times thereafter. The results were always the same. There was no pain.

I searched for the causes for this miraculous change. I could only trace those back to my altered sitting postures and my levelled shoes.

To me, this was a profound realization of the immense power of following the right technique. The wrong methods—exercises without guidance—had caused my knees to wear away. Following the right methods eventually restored them. Over time, I read all that I could about body joints and learnt a lot. Each joint has an optimum range of motion. I had been violating many of those ranges unknowingly in the past.

Thereafter, I began to blueprint the right methods for all my patterns. We probably do this cursorily, but for me this correct blueprinting meant the kind of search where you do not settle until you find methods that are right and also the best for you.

Obviously, the results were miraculous. I now had another weapon in my patterns armoury.

The right patterns—comprising right actions, thoughts, emotions and energies—that bring us the right results are at the heart of creating conscious patterns.

The woman who wants to be physically fit but binges on chocolate might come across hundreds of diets, thousands of ways of exercising, surgical procedures, pills, magic potions and even magical incantations. But which of these would be the right solution for her? Which one would actually make her fit? This is the critical question that she must answer.

You cannot expect the right results from the wrong thoughts, actions, emotions and energies, even though you might repeat them a million times.

Similarly, for the woman, following a trendy diet might not be the best solution. In 'The Mathematics of Weight Loss', a fascinating TEDx video by physicist Ruben Meerman, he shows us exactly why and how we lose fat.[36] It is simply any combination of expending more energy (exercise) and consuming less (the right things, in the right quantities). The woman must find the right combination that would help her eliminate the excess weight.

Many Indian soldiers get deployed for year-long United Nations missions in conflict-ridden countries. Such soldiers have to undergo thorough medical examinations in the beginning and at the end of the mission. I too was deployed on one such mission in the Democratic Republic of the Congo in Africa. During most of my time there, I stayed in unpolluted places, walked a lot and ate almost zero junk food, as none was available. I returned from the mission incredibly fit. A comparison of my 'before' and 'after' medical parameters is an interesting validation of the fact that getting fit or losing weight is actually straightforward if only we can get out of our surrounding unhealthy environments.

Today, finding the right methods for anything is easy! Do a Google search and you will find an oversupply of solutions on YouTube, Quora, blogging sites, etc. Or you can ask ChatGPT or any other AI tool to help you.

Keep the following points in mind before you decide to

---

[36]TEDx Talks, 'The Mathematics of Weight Loss', YouTube, 11 October 2013, https://tinyurl.com/5n94wd2u. Accessed on 22 March 2024.

follow an expert, regardless of the medium:

- Someone who has never sold anything might not be the best sales trainer. Try to learn from well-known practitioners.
- Apply common sense. Your own inner voice is the best guide. Let it speak to you.
- Test a pattern for yourself before adopting it.

'Right for You' Patterns

It is my firm belief that if our journey is painful, the goal will always seem far. So, it is our job to make things easier for ourself.

Each one of us is unique, with unique DNA and fingerprints. Our uniqueness is the nature of evolution. We forget this when we distort our own selves to become someone else.

Suppose the overweight woman tries to avoid eating chocolate by carrying an apple to eat whenever she feels the urge to binge on chocolate. But if she doesn't love apples, will she succeed? Will this beat her urge?

Here lies the simplest yet most profound key to creating and reshaping patterns. Actively look for patterns that you like, that suit you, and actively avoid patterns that do not suit you. Therefore, find things that bring you the rewards and the relief you crave.

For example, look at how one loses weight. The process should be quite straightforward. Yet, look around. The simple art of losing weight does not seem so simple. You will find most people failing at it.

If the woman's only solution to stop eating chocolate is

to carry something else, then she must carry something else that she craves for as much as a chocolate, and it should also be a healthy option at the same time.

If someone advises her to start running to lose weight, she might not do it because she is not used to running and does not like it. Prescribing a hard solution is like replacing one problem with another.

Here, we are talking about removing the perception of effort. It is we who classify things as easy or difficult, good or bad, likeable or unlikeable. What we like to do does not seem to be an effort for us.

Physics and football are neither difficult nor fun inherently. It is we who make these difficult or fun for ourselves. Make an Einstein play football and ask a Beckham to be a physicist, and both will find it hard.

Unfortunately, the word 'effort' is routinely used as a synonym for work, even though work itself is never easy or difficult, good or bad, likeable or unlikeable.

And everybody seems to be saying that 'life is hard…' I humbly disagree with this worldwide fallacy that good things must always be hard to achieve. I think that this fallacy has propagated simply because very few people in the world have put in the work needed to arrive at right-for-me methods. Most people blindly mimic someone else's approach simply because they see that person succeeding. Naturally, such work usually turns out to be hard for us. It does not suit our 'why' and 'how', or both. So, we fail and conclude that the right things must be hard.

And since a majority of us do so, societies begin to propagate this as the gospel truth—the delusion that 'life is hard!'

Nature actually works in the exact opposite manner.

Fitting a square peg in a square hole is always easy because the two are built for one another. Fitting it in any other peg will always be tougher because the peg and the hole are not built for one another. So, if you are a square peg, discover square holes for yourself.

We need patterns compatible with us, ones that are most effortless for us and fetch us the desired results. In other words, we must find patterns that fit us.

Actor Arnold Schwarzenegger won five consecutive Mr Universe titles. Schwarzenegger's approach to bodybuilding emphasized the importance of mental focus, visualization and enjoying the process of training. Of course, not everyone might enjoy it. But what matters is that he enjoyed it.

The trick to finding what works for you is to work on this problem: What takes you where you really want to go? What are the correct options of doing it? And among those correct options, which one(s) do you enjoy? What fits your lifestyle the best? What upsets your current situation the least? What gets you the most support from your environment? What gets you your rewards and relief fastest? What can you do additionally to make that enjoyable for yourself? These are the questions you must answer.

I wanted to improve my myopic vision. One exercise was to read small print and one method was to find things in small print to read.[37] Instead, I started to get my favourite books

---

[37]This technique has been suggested by Dr William Horatio Bates in his book *Perfect Sight without Glasses: The Cure of Imperfect Sight by Treatment without Glasses*, and by Dr R.S. Agarwal in his book *Mind and Vision: A Handbook for the Cure of Imperfect Sight without Glasses*. I have personally found this technique to be very effective.

photocopied in small print for my personal use. My eyesight improved. And I still read those small-print books as fast as the normal ones.

I applied the same philosophy to skills related to business, money, finance and accounting. The army had never taught us about these. So, I began to maintain the accounts of my company myself. I also found the most enjoyable books on accounts, like *Romancing the Balance Sheet* by Anil Lamba, and the most interesting accounting videos, which I could get my hands on.

You can apply this philosophy to anything. If you want to quit smoking, from the many methods available, choose the one that fits you the best. You can give up smoking by using a nicotine patch, chewing gum, not hanging out with smokers, imposing a fine on yourself, getting a coach or mentor, joining a quit-smoking group, checking yourself into a detox clinic, etc.

More than anyone else, we know what suits us best. We are unique. We must not copy others blindly. Instead, we must devise our own solutions.

It is important to remember that our patterns must also suit our biorhythms.

The TEDx talk titled 'How to Achieve Your Most Ambitious Goals' by Stephen Duneier, American professional investment manager and author, is one of the greatest examples of the power of biorhythms. This talk is also available on YouTube.[38]

Stephen discovered that he could not focus on anything for more than 5–10 minutes at a time. So, in college, he changed his

[38]Duneier, Stephen, 'How to Achieve Your Most Ambitious Goals', YouTube, https://tinyurl.com/3crtd7nd. Accessed on 23 March 2024.

approach. This is what he says in his TEDx video, 'If I would get an assignment, let's say, read five chapters in a book, I wouldn't think of it as five chapters. I wouldn't even think of it as one chapter. I would break it down into these tasks that I could achieve, that would require me to focus for just 5 or 10 minutes at a time. So, maybe three or four paragraphs. That's it.' He started breaking down all of his work into 5–10-minute slots, with breaks in between. With this technique, he went from getting C grades to being a straight A student every semester.

Using this technique, Stephen achieved his biggest goals. These included excelling in academics and business, learning new languages, auto-racing and flying, even entering the Guinness Book of World Records for creating the largest granny squares! He achieved all this simply by breaking everything into 5–10 minute slabs because he could not concentrate longer than that!

Stephen simply used his natural rhythm, rather than fighting it or trying to change himself to work the way the rest of the world wanted him to work.

As humans, we have several kinds of natural biorhythms, three of which are as follows:

- **Ultradian rhythms:** These include rhythms shorter than a day, like the work-rest rhythm described above.
- **Circadian rhythms:** These include our 24-hour daily natural rhythms, including our sleep-wake cycle.
- **Infradian rhythms:** These include rhythms lasting longer than a day, like menstruation and breeding.

Such rhythms are formed due to our patterned environment.

Ernest Rossi in *The 20 Minute Break* identified a 110-minute human activity-rest cycle, with 90 minutes of activity followed by 20 minutes of rest, during which the body recharges itself.[39] For most people, such a cycle can vary from 80–120 minutes.

This is, however, a generalization. My work-break rhythm is consistent at 45 minutes of work and 5–10 minutes of diversion. Find out what works best for you.

Similarly, whenever you cannot do something, do not simply assume that you cannot do it. Most likely, you are just using methods that do not work for you!

Finding the right methods for yourself will usually require exploration, experimentation and practice. Spend some time on it. Explore and then select the simplest, the most enjoyable and the most convenient pattern that starts giving you early rewards.

The Right Technique

'Driving a nail' might be your right method for repairing a table, but you cannot repair the table by driving the nail upside-down, no matter how hard you try. Repeatedly doing this would break the nail, or damage the table or the hammer, or hurt you.

You must learn how to drive a nail right, which is to hold it the right way up. Consider another example. For losing weight, running might be just the right pattern for you. However, you will still need to learn the right running technique, that is, how long should your strides be, how

---

[39]Rossi, Ernest Lawrence, and David Nimmons, *The 20 Minute Break: Reduce Stress, Maximize Performance, and Improve Health and Emotional Well-being Using the New Science of Ultradian Rhythms*, J.P. Tarcher, 1991.

much you should lift your feet, how you should hold your shoulders, how much you should swing your arms, whether or not to clench your hands, how to breathe, how to warm up before a run and cool down after it, etc. Again, most people do not bother about the right technique. They simply get to the 'doing' part.

Today, the internet, especially YouTube, is an excellent resource for finding the right techniques to do anything. However, there is one caution. You can optimize the amount of work that you put into something only up to a point. To complete a 10-km run, you must run 10,000 m. You cannot make it 9,999 m. But if you use the right technique, you can make running those 10,000 m as simple as it should be.

Josh Kaufman in his book, *The First 20 Hours: How to Learn Anything...Fast*, shares a simple and powerful technique to do new things fast. He also explains this through a YouTube video.[40]

Kaufman says that learning any new skill fairly well takes just 20 hours. To achieve this, he gives us four simple steps to follow:

- **Deconstruct the skill: Break down** the skill and find out exactly what comprises it. This is similar to finding root patterns. Use a good learning resource. For example, Kaufman found that most songs are played using just four chords. So, to learn to play music the fastest way possible, one must learn about these four chords first.

---

[40]Kaufman, Josh, 'The First 20 Hours: How to Learn Anything', TEDxCSU, 14 March 2013, YouTube, https://tinyurl.com/yz4zun3h. Accessed on 23 March 2024.

- **Learn enough to self-correct:** Cross the frustration barrier. For learning how to play the ukulele effortlessly, first learn how to produce some tune on it.
- **Remove practice barriers:** Remove distracting activities and emotional barriers from your routine.
- **Practise:** Try practising for at least 20 hours.

Using this technique, Kaufman began playing songs on the ukulele fairly well, and that too in just about 20 hours!

American author Tim Ferriss provides similar advice on finding the right technique to learn something easily. His two techniques are reproduced below. These rules are similar to Josh Kaufman's *The First 20 Hours*:

- DiSSS:[41]
    - **Di for Deconstruction:** Deconstruct the skill into useful units of knowledge. For example, to learn how to juggle three balls, these learnable units can be: (a) what kind of juggling balls to use, (b) how to stand while juggling, (c) how to position your hands while juggling, (d) where to look, (e) how to hold the balls, (f) when and how to toss them, (g) how to catch them back, etc.
    - **S for Selection:** Which 20 per cent of those units of knowledge will lead to 80 per cent of the results? For juggling three balls, the critical minimum units could be (a) learning when to toss the second ball when the first one is already in the air (the right moment is when the first ball starts descending) and

[41]Ferriss, Tim, 'The Art and Science of Learning Anything Faster', *Tim Ferriss*, https://tinyurl.com/s8hj5t22. Accessed on 23 March 2024.

(b) learning where to look while juggling (never at your hands, but always at the balls).

  - **S for Sequencing:** What is the most effective order for learning these units? For learning how to juggle three balls, you can first toss one ball between both hands, then two balls between both hands at the right moments, and finally three balls between both hands, continuing to focus on when to release a ball and where to look.
  - **S for Stakes:** Determine the psychological or social stakes you set up for instilling discipline and motivation in yourself. This is the same as creating rewards or disincentives.
- CaFE:[42]
  - **Ca for Compression:** Compress the most important 20 per cent learning units into an awesome cheat sheet.
  - **F for Frequency:** Set up a frequency of practising, based on the goal and your personal limits.
  - **E for Encoding:** Encoding involves creating mental anchors to remember the first 20 per cent units that you must learn. For instance, when learning to play the guitar, mastering four chords—G, C, D and E minor—is part of the first 20 per cent of the learning units. To recall these chords, you could use a mnemonic like 'Giant Cats Dance Elegantly', where each word represents one of the chords that you must learn.

---

[42]Ibid.

The right techniques of doing things can make you like them. Wrong techniques, on the other hand, rarely lead to enjoyment.

Earliest Results

If we get the results we desire, we do more and our patterns get reinforced. If we do not get the results we hope for, we do less and the concerned pattern gets curbed.

For example, once a smoker experiences the results of not smoking, like no shortness of breath, better stamina, and improved life, he starts sticking to those patterns. This is one of the examples of when patterns start moving from consciousness to subconsciousness.

Criticality of the 'Right Blueprints' for Patterns

Here is a well-known fable about Mulla Nasruddin, a character from Middle Eastern and Central Asian folklore known for his humorous and insightful anecdotes.

> Late one night, a man heading home from work found Mulla Nasruddin searching feverishly for something under a streetlight.
>
> 'What are you looking for, Nasruddin?' the man asked.
>
> 'I dropped my keys on my way home today!' replied Narsuddin, without looking up.
>
> The man was puzzled, 'But why here, Nasruddin? The road leading to your home is over there.'
>
> 'Oh, but the light is better here!'

This fable is often interpreted as a commentary on how people tend to focus on what's familiar or convenient rather than what's actually needed or important. It highlights the tendency to choose the seemingly easier path, even if it doesn't lead to the solution.

The irony is that the right path or the right solution is always the shortest or the easiest one, even if one has to make or buy a torch for it. Look at the story of Nasruddin. Had he chosen to buy a torch, he would have found his keys and been back home in no time.

What causes us to adopt whatever comes our way instead of seeking the right patterns? The most common explanation is that we humans love to stick to our 'comfort zones'. A comfort zone is nothing but an existing pattern that has outlived its utility. Anything within that zone seems easier to us and anything outside it seems like an effort. This is a classic example of patterns without conscious thought.

Venturing into the unknown involves risk, and our brains are wired to avoid perceived threats. Risk aversion is an evolutionary pattern that helps ensure our survival.

The comfort zone is, therefore, a familiar and predictable environment, within which we feel in control and experience lower levels of stress and anxiety. But getting into a comfort zone to get away from necessary change is certainly not the conscious application of patterns. The conscious application of patterns involves the conscious awareness of why we do what we do. The moment we become aware of such patterns and their consequences, we become able to turn away from such thoughtless and false comfort. And then we begin to seek the right patterns, which eventually lead us to where we wish to go.

Should We Look for the Perfect 'Right Patterns'?

'There is beauty and humility in imperfection.'

—Guillermo del Toro, Mexican filmmaker

In his book *Thinking, Fast and Slow*, author Daniel Kahneman, a Nobel Prize-winning psychologist, discusses various cognitive biases and heuristics that can affect decision-making processes. In particular, he explores the concept of 'analysis paralysis', where excessive deliberation and consideration of options can lead to decision-making difficulties and poorer outcomes.

So, do not wait to find the perfect technique or pattern. At some point, preferably early on, start 'doing'. Then observe, think and self-correct. Perfection is a trap. Volume, not perfection, is the solution. Perfection comes automatically after you do a volume of work.

12

BERT 2: Enable Your Patterns

'Give me a lever long enough and a fulcrum on which to place it, and I shall move the world.'

—Archimedes, physicist and mathematician

A friend recently said, 'Ever since my wife and I moved into our new house, we have started going for a walk daily.'

This is an example of one's environment enabling activities. Enablement means creating or placing enablers to facilitate patterns, removing impediments that make those patterns difficult and creating disruptors to disrupt any negative patterns.

Such enablers could be in our environment or within us. For example, placing a glass of water by the bedside can enable us to start the next day by consuming a glass of water. Similarly, taking two deep breaths when angry acts as a disruptor, disrupting the pattern of anger and enabling us to regain control.

Let Go and Reduce Clutter

George Armitage Miller, well-known American psychologist, is famous for his seminal paper titled 'The Magical Number Seven, Plus or Minus Two: Some Limits on Our Capacity for Processing Information'.[43] In this work, Miller refers to the channel capacity of humans as the cognitive limit for processing and retaining information in short-term memory. Miller suggests that individuals can typically hold around seven (plus or minus two) chunks of information in their short-term memory at a time. For example, when trying to remember a phone number (e.g., 308-4345), the average person can easily recall the seven digits because it falls within the typical channel capacity of short-term memory.

Miller concludes, 'There seems to be some limitation built into us either by learning or by the design of our nervous systems, a limit that keeps our channel capacities in this general range.'

So, if we hear different tones, we can distinguish up to six or seven of them, beyond which we fail at telling them apart. If we see clusters of dots flashed on a screen, we can correctly guess their number up to five to nine dots, after which we get confused. If we see different objects, we can classify them easily in about five to nine categories, but beyond that we find it difficult.

British biological anthropologist Robin Dunbar created a formula for similarly predicting the average size of groups in which various animal species live, based on the size of the

[43]Miller, George A., 'The Magical Number Seven, Plus or Minus Two: Some Limits on Our Capacity for Processing Information', *Psychological Review*, Vol. 63, No. 2, 1956, pp. 81–97, https://tinyurl.com/3pycfkkm. Accessed on 22 April 2024.

neocortex of their brains.[44] For humans, that number is 147.8, or approximately 150! An average human can maintain close relationships with up to a maximum of around 150 people, at one given point in time.

Malcolm Gladwell cites the above studies in his book *The Tipping Point.* He also quotes the evolutionary biologist S.L. Washburn, who similarly said, 'Man evolved to feel strongly about few people, short distances, and relatively brief intervals of time, and these are still dimensions of life that are important to him.'[45]

Under all our capacities, there is energy, and if that energy has limits—even if those limits are massive—our capacities must have limits, too.

We must acknowledge such human limitations by reducing the clutter and disorganization around us. We must limit the number of things that our bodies, minds, emotions and energies can deal with at any point in time. This will make our world more sensible and predictable to us. As a result, we will have more energy to be creative and productive.

The simplest solution to getting more organized is to let go. Here is an example of how simple letting go is and yet how difficult most people find it.

---

[44]Dunbar, R.I.M., 'Neocortex Size as a Constraint on Group Size in Primates', *Journal of Human Evolution*, Vol. 22, No. 6, 1992, pp. 469–93.

[45]Gladwell, Malcolm, *The Tipping Point: How Little Things Can Make a Big Difference*, Little, Brown and Company, 2000.

In time gone by, a man went to his king.

'Life has given me nothing, your majesty,' he complained, 'even though I have worked so hard!'

The wise king asked the man to come back the next morning. Next morning, the king asked the man to start running. 'All the land, till the farthest point that you can touch, will be yours. There is only one condition. You have to be back before the sun sets or else you will lose everything that you have gained.'

The man was overjoyed. He began to run. By mid-day, he had covered quite a few miles. But he was greedy.

Let me run a little more, he thought. So he ran some more and more.

By the time he turned back to return, the sun was setting. The man sprinted as hard as he could, to the point of collapsing, but in vain. The sun set before he could reach back. He ended where he had started—with nothing.

Our daily race is similar to this man's. We want to ace them all, mostly because we want to miss out on nothing that others also want. So, we go after everything and by the end of each day we end up gaining almost nothing.

Thus, it is always better to go after limited things, ones that fit our channel capacities. We can also use our channel capacities intelligently to expand our limits. For example, we can divide something we need to do into five to nine separate categories. Then we can create another five to nine sub-categories under each one of the pre-existing categories, and so on if needed.

In reality, we do things like this often, without realizing the underlying reason. For example, most of us memorize a 10-digit phone number by splitting it into two or more parts.

Defaults, Triggers, Rewards and Disruptors

'Every body continues to be in its state of rest or of uniform motion in a straight line unless compelled by some external force to act otherwise.'

—Isaac Newton, physicist

> Sam and Anita had a hearty dinner and called for the bill.
>
> When Sam checked the bill, he saw an extra charge printed. It read 'Donation to Missionaries of ABC Charity - $1.00*. This $1.00 will be donated to the Missionaries of ABC Charity on your behalf. Please let us know if you wish this amount to be removed from your bill, and it will be deleted.'
>
> *What a lovely way to rip off someone else to fund your own charities!* thought Sam. However, it was too much effort to ask the waiter to remove that amount. Besides, it was just a dollar. So, Sam and Anita just paid and left.

We often stick with defaults because changing them requires effort, and this applies to patterns as well. For example, consider moving your TV from your bedroom to your living room to reduce night-time TV watching. By default, your night-time TV viewing decreases because returning to your old pattern would require moving the TV back or adjusting your sleeping arrangement, both of which require extra effort.

My wife and I bought a flat with a spacious balcony facing the rising sun. What could be a better, healthier and more fulfilling start to each day than sitting quietly in such a balcony, soaking in the early morning sun and working even before the rest of the world woke up? And since we lived in such a home, it became much easier for us to adopt these patterns that were beneficial for us in the long run.

Create as many defaults as you can to drive the patterns you want to see in your life. For example, in patterning your business, identify and hack away at all needless processes. Only keep the ones that support and power your key outcomes and make them easy for your employees.

Consider another example. If you believe that relationships 'suck', you can reshape your environment by surrounding yourself with friends who are in great relationships. This will help you alter your belief.

In a lighter vein, to lose weight, you could live on a higher floor with no lift and take the stairs each day!

Fig. 12.1: Use the power of inertia

Triggers, too, can set off the patterns you want. Just make those triggers 'sticky', so that they grab your attention and push you to do something.

In *The Tipping Point*, Gladwell tells us that all things can be made to stick: 'There is a simple way of packaging information that, under the right circumstances, can make it irresistible', he writes. 'All you have to do is find it.'[46] He further writes, 'If you paid careful attention to the structure and format of your material, you could dramatically enhance stickiness.'

Gladwell cites an experiment by social psychologist Howard Levanthal in the 1960s, in which groups of college students at Yale University were handed out different pamphlets on tetanus inoculation.[47] The aim was to make them take those free vaccinations at the campus health centre.

To see what worked best, Howard tried various modifications to the pamphlet. Most modifications, like adding photos showing the consequences of not taking the tetanus shots, made little difference to the number of students actually getting vaccinated.

But then, the experimenters simply included a map of the university with the location of the health centre circled, along with the timings at which the shots could be taken listed on the pamphlet. The number of students who visited the health centre and got those shots increased dramatically! Once the information became practical and personal, the students acted on it.

As humans, we are primed to react to human cues.

Ultimately, how you personalize your triggers depends on what works best for you. If you are visual, a picture of a smiling child might work for you and make you smile. Another person might be triggered by the company of a smiling person. A third one might respond to abstractions.

---

[46]Gladwell, Malcolm, *The Tipping Point: How Little Things Can Make a Big Difference*, Little, Brown and Company, 2000.
[47]Ibid.

But make your triggers default, sticky and human. Let each trigger tell you what is in it for you and what exactly you must do. Here are some examples:

- My wife puts up a daily quote in her kitchen. It is her daily positivity reminder.

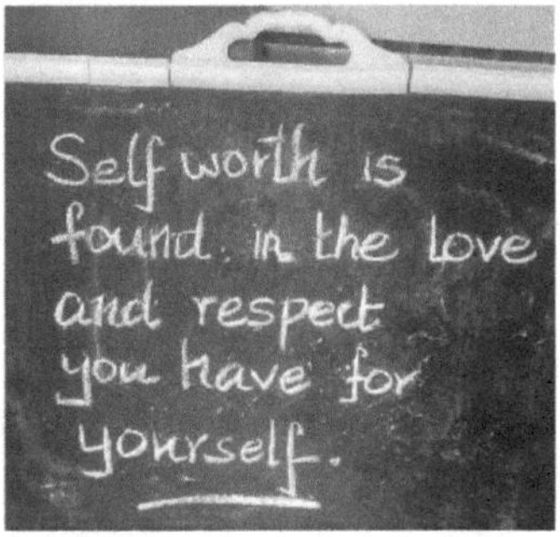

Fig. 12.2: My wife Archana's message board in her kitchen acts as a cue for her daily dose of positivity

- A friend puts up everything he learns—or wants to learn—on charts. He refers to them as he goes about his work. This is why vision boards work. We begin to subconsciously follow what we put there.
- Atul Gawande in *The Checklist Manifesto* advocates usage of checklists to list out what we must do, so as not to forget or miss out on something.[48]
- Alcoholics Anonymous works so well because people and groups are powerful human triggers. Joining forces with similar-thinking people or getting a mentor also helps.

---

[48]Gawande, Atul, *The Checklist Manifesto: How to Get Things Right*, Penguin, 2009.

- I myself use custom hand-painted messages on coasters, a notebook by my bedside, boards, pictures and items placed at particular spots as triggers.

Rewards, too, are great triggers. We like doing things that can get us something pleasurable or lead us towards rewards. While doing so, we should keep the following things in mind:

- Link rewards directly to the patterns they drive. A reward is powerful if you can attain it on performing the pattern linked to it. That smoothie with which you reward yourself after a run is powerful only if it is available to you after you run. If you can have it anytime you want, its power to drive your running will disappear.
- Make rewards immediate. The armed forces understand the power of immediate rewards. In the leadership book *Turn The Ship Around!*, author L. David Marquet, captain, US navy (retd), writes, 'Immediate recognition means just that, immediate. Not thirty days, not thirty minutes. It should be immediate.'[49] A pattern's cause-effect connection to a reward blurs if the reward follows too late.
- Extrinsic rewards alone cannot drive performance. A pattern driven by an extrinsic reward, like a run driven by a smoothie, stops the moment you stop the reward. Instead, intrinsic rewards, like feeling good after running, drive patterns over the long term. So, employ external rewards as starters or catalysts. For example, when you start learning music and it is not

---

[49]Marquet, L. David, *Turn the Ship Around: How to Create Leadership at Every Level*, Greenleaf Book Group Press, 2012.

fun, use a reward till the point the learning exercise becomes pleasurable for you.

- Existing great patterns, too, can be used as rewards. If you love fruit, reward yourself with a healthy fruit after a run. This is one good pattern driving another.
- Keep changing your patterns and rewards to avoid boredom. So, the woman who wants to be fit could alternate walking with friends, cycling and dancing, all of which she presumably likes. Again, novelty alone will not drive your patterns.

Suppose you have decided to learn how to dance. Create as many triggers as you can to enable this. Put up pictures of yourself dancing. Create and play a collection of your favourite dance music. Buy dancing shoes. Join a dance group. Find a dance partner who you enjoy dancing with. Watch dance movies. Enter a dance competition!

Similarly, try to stay away from existing triggers that set off patterns that you do not want in your life. It might be a time trigger, like feeling distracted before lunch. It might simply be a person, someone you cannot remain calm around.

Once you have identified such triggers, this is what you can do:

- Question why those triggers set you off. The best method is to remove the underlying root causes.
- Remove negative triggers. Throw out those chocolates, remove the TV from your bedroom, hide the remote in a drawer, etc.
- You can replace the negative triggers with others that lead to different patterns. To avoid watching TV for long hours, keep an interesting book next to your bed.

- Prepare and arm yourself against unwanted triggers popping up. Carry a little pocket card to remind yourself not to be defensive around someone. Let the screen saver on your computer screen remind you that you are awesome.
- You cannot always avoid negative triggers, like a place you must go to or a person you must work with. In such cases, you can use disruptors. A pistol or rifle has a safety catch to prevent it from going off. You can create your own safety catches to apply the needed brakes on your pre-scripted responses, give your logical mind the needed time to step in, and for your illogical emotions to ebb.
  - Two deep breaths is the best disruption for most unconscious patterns. Usually, our conscious brain gets bypassed when we encounter powerful triggers. Two breaths will give you a break and also supply your brain with oxygen. That will help put your thinking brain back into action, to check your illogical reactions.
  - Mel Robbins in her book, *The 5 Second Rule*, introduces another kind of disruption.[50] She tells us to count backwards from 5 to 0, and on reaching 0, we should do just the thing that we are hesitating to do! This works pretty well.
  - Memory expert Anthony Metivier shares two easily remembered questions to silence negative thoughts: 'Are my thoughts useful?' and 'How do they behave?'[51]

---

[50]Robbins, Mel, *The 5 Second Rule*, Post Hill Press, 2017.

[51]TEDx Talks, 'Two Easily Remembered Questions That Silence Negative

- When hidden triggers catch us by surprise, we forget to take even those two deep breaths. We forget to count from 5 to 0. The trick is to mock-practise two deep breaths and mock-count 5 to 0 in advance. Practise this till it becomes a pattern. If you practise it, the disruptor comes into play naturally when needed.

Keep experimenting till you find suitable disruptors for yourself. The key is to align all of these—your patterns and your rewards—to get the desired results.

Full-Kit, Batch and Anchor

In manufacturing, you start the production of a batch of goods only after ensuring that everything—raw materials, tools, manpower, etc.—is available and will not fall short midway. Failing to ensure this full-kitting leads to a halt in production midway and efficiency plummets. Eliyahu Goldratt talks about this in his bestselling book *Theory of Constraints*.[52]

Ensure similar full-kitting for everything required to support your patterns because patterns, too, should be extremely convenient for us. Any brakes that could disrupt your desired patterns must be removed.

Gather all the tools needed. If you want to cycle, get your bicycle in shape and find places you would like to cycle to. Join a cycling club. Or find a partner! Similarly, if you want to get support to give up smoking, find and join a group of

---

Thoughts | Anthony Metivier | TEDxDocklands', YouTube, https://tinyurl.com/52c5ye55. Accessed on 23 March 2024.

[52]Goldratt, E.M., *What is this Thing Called Theory of Constraints and How Should it be Implemented?*, Gower Publishing Company, 1990.

non-smokers who can motivate you.

In manufacturing, we batch similar things to be manufactured together. Similarly, we can also batch similar patterns together. If you batch patterns together, their power compounds.

People batch the calls they need to return for certain times of the day, schedule meetings on certain days of the week, certain actions at the end of each month, etc. Similar tasks become easier, more actionable and more efficient when grouped together.

The bottom line is to organize whatever we need in order to minimize efforts needed to aid the formation of our patterns. But whenever we set up new triggers, we tend to miss or bypass the triggers when they are most needed. This is because our old patterns are still strong and drag us back to our old routines. We can solve this by anchoring or linking our patterns to our already established routines. An anchor holds a ship in place in the sea. Whenever currents try to drift it elsewhere, the anchor pulls the ship back.

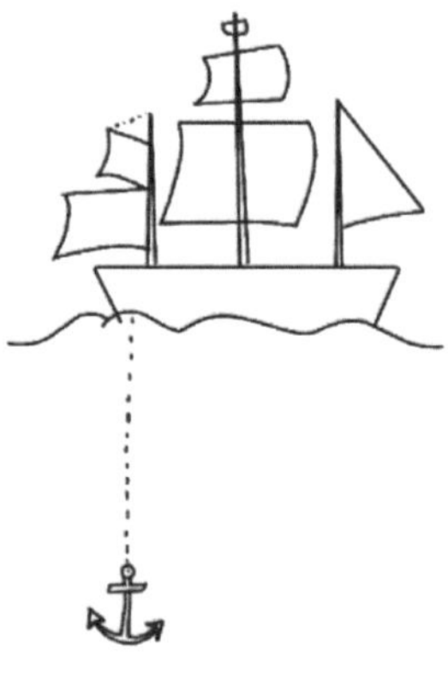

Fig. 12.3: An anchored ship

Similarly, when we anchor our new patterns to existing routines, those routines in turn help us put our new patterns into action.

To be effective, anchors must:

- Already be a part of your routine
- Be within your control; the time of the day, like morning or late night, that is totally within your control acts as a great anchor
- Be difficult to overlook
- Be easy to replicate or take along if you change locations

Here are some examples of effective anchors:

- **Time anchors**
    - Days of the week: Monday morning checklists work fabulously. Being the first day of the week, it is the easiest to control and plan. For some, Fridays might be a better option. My Tuesdays and Wednesdays are out-of-office-meeting days. So, I can plan and batch meetings in advance. Similarly, Wednesdays and Saturdays are grooming mornings, so that I don't ever miss trimming my nails and hair.
    - Time slots during the day: The time slots that you can control are great anchors, too. They come around each day! This is why early morning and night rituals are so powerful. Wake up with a smile, have gratitude in your heart, drink a glass of water in the morning, do breathing exercises, meditate, enjoy some quiet time, plan and visualize the day ahead. Similarly, at night, review your day and plan ahead and write in your journal. You can also select from other times, like breakfast,

lunch or dinner, the drive to your office, the first 15 minutes after reaching and before leaving your workplace, the way back home, the time when you reach home, etc.
    - Other repetitive periods, like the start or end of a month, quarterly or annual routines, are also good.
- **Place anchors:** The entrance to your home, your work-desk, the refrigerator door—all are great place anchors.
- **Event anchors:** Meetings, work trips, parties, drives, holidays, etc., can be great event anchors.
- **Routines you never miss:** These are things that define you, like your coffee mug, your work desk, etc. For me, my study room at home, my office board and my habit of waking up early are powerful anchors. To these, I anchor many things, because these are patterns that I rarely miss.

13

BERT 3: Rhythmize Your Patterns

'Success is neither magical nor mysterious. Success is the natural consequence of consistently applying the basic fundamentals.'

—Jim Rohn, motivational speaker

Once we have designed the right patterns for ourselves and enabled them, we must build them into the rhythms of our life. After all, that is the only way that they will play out.

Repetitions and Drama

Everything about us functions like a muscle—our limbs, mind, emotions, willpower, courage, gratitude, networking, financial planning, ideas, etc. Just like muscles, they all grow stronger through repetitive use.

> Many years ago, a great king was mighty pleased with a mathematician in his kingdom. The king deemed the mathematician to be the greatest in the world. The king commanded him to wish for whatever he desired. The mathematician smiled and asked for grains of wheat, as many as the 64 squares of a chessboard. There was one condition. He requested for the grains to be doubled each time one moved from one square to the next.
>
> The king laughed. He commanded that the mathematician's wish be fulfilled.
>
> A chessboard was brought. The king's men counted one grain for the first square, two for the second, four for the third, and so on, doubling the number each time.
>
> They could not reach even close to the sixty-fourth square. To reach that square, assuming each grain of wheat weighed 30 milligrams, they would have needed approximately 553,410 trillion metric tons of wheat!

The power of compounded repetitions is immense.

Earlier, we dispelled one argument against repetitions—that repetitions kill our creativity. We saw how repetitive patterns actually support our creativity by giving us the freedom to think and create. Another argument against repetition is that adults find repetition boring. But that too is incorrect.

Gladwell writes that pre-schoolers do not find repetition boring. He says, 'They (pre-schoolers) are surrounded by stuff they don't understand—things that are novel. So the driving force for pre-schoolers is not a search for novelty, like it is with older kids, it's a search for understanding and predictability.'[53] He further says, 'By predicting what is going to happen, I think they feel a real sense of affirmation and self-worth.'[54]

Basically, children seek patterns, just the way we do to solve things that we find complex. This is why we read self-help books and attend self-help workshops.

In creating conscious patterns, our repetitions are again driven by the need to understand and master. Of course, if our brains do not understand why we are following a pattern and if our emotions tell us that whatever we are doing is useless, we will surely be bored! If we know where our patterns are leading us, they will excite us. Arnold Schwarzenegger never felt bored while pumping iron because he knew that this was making him like his icon, Reg Park, a former Mr Universe and a well-known actor.

So, be like a child while designing your patterns, infusing them with curiosity and wonder about where they are taking you. In addition, you can also alternate between similar patterns that excite you and get you the same results.

In this regard, I find one technique particularly powerful and revealing for beginners looking to reshape their patterns. You can build a daily, 10-minute routine in which you repeat five selected patterns, each for just two minutes, including the time taken to switch over from one pattern to another. For example, use each pattern to shape your environment, body, mind, emotions and an action. It could be exercising (for example, two suryanamaskar reps or 10 pull-ups), organizing

---

[53]Gladwell, Malcolm, *The Tipping Point: How Little Things Can Make a Big Difference*, Little, Brown and Company, 2000, p. 125.

[54]Ibid. 126.

your stuff (shaping your environment), meditating, observing your emotion(s) and journaling. This exercise also demonstrates the importance you attach to these five things because if you are not able to spare even 10 minutes each day for these—your carefully selected patterns in life—then your problem is not time management or these patterns. You will then be forced to acknowledge that either you must put more thought into reshaping those patterns till they pull you towards themselves, or you need to dig deeper to discover what lies beneath the avoidance, or check whether these patterns or their outcomes are truly important to you, or if you are just fooling yourself and want to do them simply because someone else has told you that you should want to do them.

This exercise will also force you to 'set up' in advance for the patterns you seek. If you want to journal for just two minutes a day, your journal and a working pen better be within easy reach; same goes for other patterns.

Once you get used to these patterns, you can move them from your 10-minute slot to your life rhythms.

Drama and repetition are two ends of the same scale. Sometimes, in order to change, we must repeat a thing many times. And sometimes, a single dramatic instance causes us to change!

A smoker can give up smoking gradually, or he can declare to his girlfriend dramatically, on an impulse, 'If you marry me, I will quit smoking!'

Drama is just a word to highlight the significance that we attach to something. Dramatic events can have a huge impact on us. A traumatic event, like the death of a parent, can convert a truant child into a responsible person overnight. Extreme happiness can cause such effects, too—a new father vowing to stop drinking! Another example can be some people choosing to declare publicly what they want to achieve.

To understand how much something should be repeated, look at this graph:

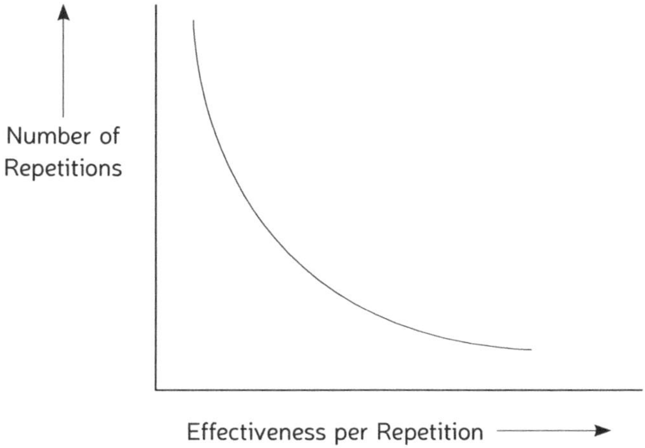

Fig. 13.1: Number of repetitions versus effectiveness per repetition (If each repetition is less effective, you'll need to do more repetitions to achieve the same result)

Suppose you exercise for 10 minutes, and each 10-minute routine strengthens a particular muscle of yours by 0.1 per cent. This means that to increase your muscle strength by 1 per cent, you must repeat that exercise 10 times, and to bring about a 10 per cent change, you must repeat it 100 times.

This is only a simplistic example to illustrate that the number of repetitions needed depends on the effectiveness per repetition and the results that you want. To get the same result, if the effectiveness per repetition of a certain pattern is low, you have to repeat it more times.

However, the relationship between the number of

repetitions and the effects is not linear. It is actually a curve (as seen in Fig. 13.2).

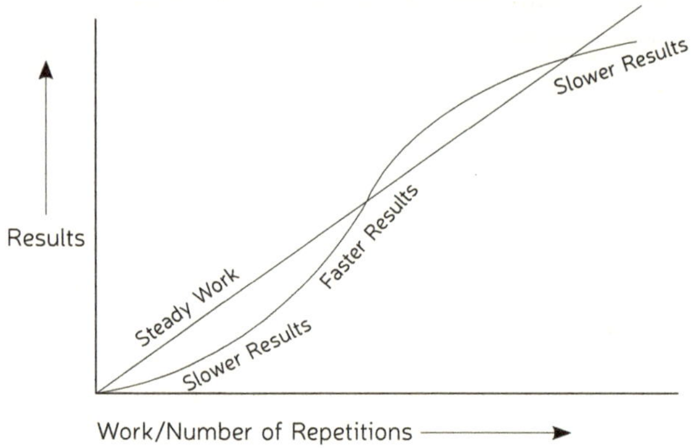

Fig. 13.2: Number of repetitions of a pattern versus results

In addition, with every repetition, we also evolve our patterns, such that with every repetition, the outcome per repetition also increases. As per Daniel Coyle, the author of *Talent Code*, a 4 per cent improvement in learning with each repetition is the optimum percentage at which we should increase the degree of 'difficulty' of our patterns to get to the desired results the fastest.

This sounds logical. However, the phrase 'degree of difficulty' can be replaced with 'degree of complexity' because difficulty is a subjective experience.

Imagine learning a musical instrument through repetition. As you start playing that instrument, you first focus on producing simple sounds from it. As you progress, you progressively increase the degree of complexity of those sounds.

Now, someone who truly loves music most likely experiences that increase in complexity in the form of excitement. However, someone who is learning music merely to impress someone might experience the same increase in complexity as increased frustration and difficulty, as getting to the end result is all that matters to this person.

It is important to make the distinction here. If a pattern starts becoming difficult for you, you should work on locating the cause and removing it. Otherwise, your patterns might not work for you.

Fig. 13.2 shows that initially, a new pattern takes more time to produce results, as it takes more time to create the foundation. So, when we start to repeat something, initially the results are hard to be noticed. But once the foundation is ready, building on it becomes easier. As we continue, the results become more and more perceptible.

Ultimately, the curve of the results begins to flatten out again. This happens because we start approaching the limits of the results that are achievable through the concerned pattern. To enhance the results further, we have to adopt some new pattern or increase the complexity of that pattern.

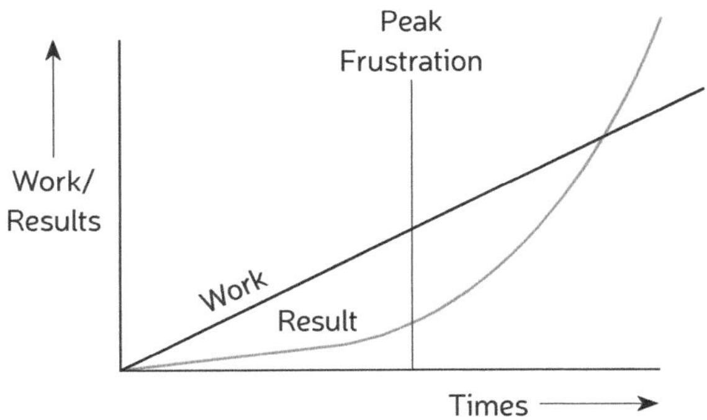

Fig. 13.3: Initial lack of results from a pattern can lead to an early peak of frustration

Understanding how repetitions work is crucial when it comes to using patterns well. If we do not understand the initial lack of results, we will experience a peak of frustration early on and will tend to give up. At this stage, perseverance and careful planning are needed to get past this peak and start getting results.

Do you recall the techniques of DiSSS and CaFE? Both techniques aim to help one get quick results to overcome this valley of impatience at the start of any new learning.

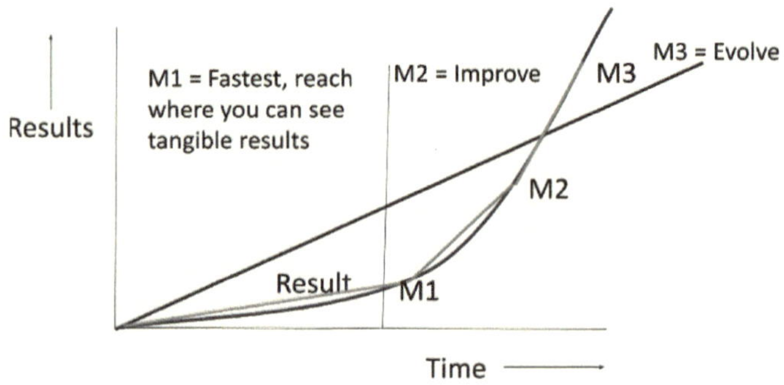

Fig. 13.4: In the initial phase (M1) of pattern repetition, focus on quick results for motivation. Then aim for continuous improvement (M2). Finally, modify and evolve the pattern for even better results (M3).

As shown in the figure above, in the beginning, we try to find the fastest way to reach the point at which we start seeing tangible results. Thereafter, we improve and evolve.

Similarly, if we do not understand the flattening of the curve of results once we end up sticking to a pattern long enough, we tend to become frustrated again. This, however, is only a signal that we are nearing the limit of what a pattern can provide us, and that we need to make some changes.

'Dovetail' and 'Parallel Process'

In the movie *Enter The Dragon* (1973), actor Bruce Lee is shown sailing in a small dhow to take part in a martial arts tournament on a privately owned island in Hong Kong. Other participants, too, are travelling on the same dhow. One of those participants, a bully, is tormenting the boys on the dhow. He is clearly spoiling for a fight.

Soon, this participant swaggers over to where Bruce Lee is sitting and asks, 'What's your style?'

Bruce answers, 'My style? You can call it the art of fighting without fighting.'

The bully challenges Bruce Lee to fight him. Bruce points to a nearby island where they would get more space to fight. Then he tricks the bully into boarding the dhow's safety boat first, to get to that island. Once the bully is in that boat, Lee quickly hands the safety boat's rope to the kids whom the man had been bullying. The kids are gleeful! They exact their revenge by pulling the rope to rock and flood the safety boat, while that man tries to save himself from falling overboard!

Bruce Lee watches the fun, having demonstrated his art of fighting without fighting, without even raising a finger!

Dovetailing and parallel processing are like the art of fighting without fighting. By using these techniques, we make our patterns play out without adding any significant work or time to our existing routines. Dovetailing means inserting a new thing into what we already do, without letting the original routine get substantially affected.

In another movie, *Over the Top* (1987), action hero Sylvester Stallone plays the role of a trailer driver preparing for the US Arm Wrestling Championship. In the movie, he has a spring-loaded arm fitted inside the driving cabin of his trailer. While he drives, he keeps exercising his arm too, using that fixture! This might neither be advisable nor permitted, but it is a great example of effective dovetailing.

The best method of dovetailing is to combine something that seems like an effort to you with something that absorbs you. We learnt this as cadets in the military academy. As army cadets, we often underwent long, gruelling marches, with heavy packs on our backs. During most such marches, one of my closest friends and I would crack jokes for hours on end. This was fun and often made us forget the weight of the heavy packs on our backs. Often we had no memory of the effort being put into those marches. We were too busy guffawing at those stupid jokes.

Even today, to increase my body's flexibility, I often sit in a particular position and get to work. Often, when that work is important, I have no memory or feeling of the effort involved in sitting in that pose because of the absorbing nature of the work. In such situations, one's body does not even register the effort involved. The action that we dovetail with our absorbing work becomes a subconscious activity.

At its best, dovetailing is like Mr Han (the character played by the martial artist Jackie Chan) in yet another Hollywood movie, *The Karate Kid* (the 2010 remake of the original movie). Han is teaching Xiao Dre, a cocky young American kid, the basics of kung fu. At one point in the movie, Xiao angrily flings his jacket to the ground. Mr Han makes Xiao pick up his jacket, wear it, take it off, fling it down again, then pick it up, and repeat this routine over and over again, for days. After complying and doing this hundreds of times, Xiao gives up and yells, 'This is stupid. I am done!'

At this point, Mr Han demonstrates to Xiao how, in the guise of teaching him manners through picking up his jacket, he also taught him a karate block that requires exactly the same body movements!

If you sing as you take a bath, if you talk on the phone as you walk your dog or discuss something important with a friend as you walk, or listen to an audio tape while you drive, you are dovetailing.

Fig. 13.5: Dovetailing

I absolutely love dovetailing. I dovetailed my eye exercises into my daily routines by doing the following:

- Sipping tea in the morning sunlight (which is great for eyesight)
- Using an eye-patch to cover one eye at a time while

working or reading something (this helped me exercise each eye)

- Palming and splashing my closed eyes with water during work breaks
- Adopting a convenient yoga posture for sitting while working

You, too, can dovetail desired patterns into your daily routines. Here are some examples:

- Cycling or walking to work (exercise)
- Alternating between sitting cross-legged (knees flexed inwards) and with your knees flexed outwards while working. This is excellent for strengthening your knees, thighs and calves, without lifting a finger.
- Using a treadmill work-desk (a business partner used to do this)
- Using a stress ball while talking on the phone (exercising your fingers)
- Eating meals together, dancing together, playing together as a family
- Combining work, travel and fun. Many professionals do this. My wife and I often travel together for work assignments. We explore the place, and I set aside a few days solely for work. If possible, we also take stops en route to extend our travels.

Parallel processing and dovetailing are very similar. But parallel processing uses multiple energies—yours or others'—to run things in parallel. This is like cooking two dishes together, but on two different gas burners.

Parallel processing does not mean splitting the same energy

between multiple tasks. It is just the clever and simultaneous use of multiple resources. Successful people parallel-process all the time; they hire, automate, delegate, collaborate, outsource, crowdsource, etc., to get as many things done as possible.

- Delegate work to your staff. Hire an executive assistant to do things you should not be doing. Hire a driver. Delegate investment decisions to a financial adviser. Outsource non-key business activities to partners. By doing this, you build routines where others do some of your work, while you focus on something else.
- The internet has many outsourcing options, like Fiverr, Upwork and TaskRabbit. At these sites, you pay someone else to do repetitive work that you do not want to do yourself. And when you pay someone, that person is bound to do the allotted work.
- Automate whatever can be done automatically. For example, you can instruct your bank to automatically invest a certain amount each month, use an AI (artificial intelligence) chatbot to answer product-related queries from potential buyers, set automated reminders, etc.

Parallel processing just needs initial planning and setting-up. For example, for automating investments you need to find a great investment manager once, who then takes on this repetitive work.

Many people fear losing control and hence are bad at delegating and letting go. They are often bad at parallel processing. Such people get limited to using their own energies and capabilities.

Summing it up, learn to focus on your repetitive thoughts,

emotions, actions and surroundings. Do it till these routines get pushed to your subconscious and become automatic. Only then will they become powerful, meaningful patterns that ceaselessly power you.

14

BERT 4: Tinker with Your Patterns

'I have not failed. I've just found 10,000 ways that won't work.'

—Thomas Edison, inventor

Once we get the hang of creating our own patterns, the real fun begins. We start tinkering, experimenting, checking out the results and making changes accordingly. Most of this happens subconsciously.

From Unconscious Incompetence to Awareness of Unconscious Competence

Once we fashion a pattern, we must usually tinker with it till we get comfortable with it. For example, if we start journalling, we might alter what, when, where and how we journal till we get it right. This is natural.

Further, as we shape our patterns, we move from a state of unconscious incompetence to one of awareness or consciousness of our unconscious competence.

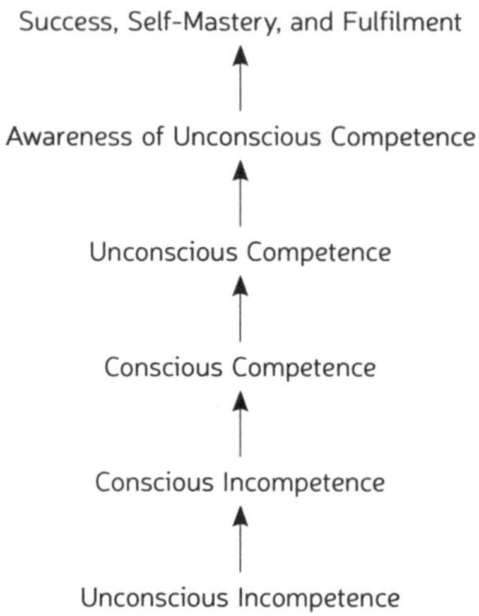

Fig. 14.1: See how conscious patterns take you from unconscious incompetence to self-mastery, success and fulfilment

How Many?

We have thousands, maybe millions, of patterns. Most serve us excellently. There are a few that we must change. By letting go and decluttering our lives, we minimize these too.

Of the patterns that we want to change, how many can we pick up at one time? Should we tackle them all together or sequentially, one at a time?

Working on multiple patterns at a time is important. For example, when we get our car repaired, we do not get it repaired in parts. For the car to work well, all essential parts must function properly.

For us too, some things are basic and too important to park and leave for later. Our body, mind, emotions, actions and environment must all function together and that too synchronously. We cannot set any of these aside and hope that our life will work in its entirety.

Similarly, our health, basic finances, relationships, etc., must go hand in hand. Neglect one and all else suffers. A friend with a successful business has ruined his health to such an extent that he now shuttles in and out of hospitals. His wealth is not compensating for his health in any manner.

Our body is the perfect example of such parallel functioning. It runs all essential patterns together. The digestive system digests, the lungs function, the heart pumps, the brain works. There is no conflict. Everything works simultaneously, independently and interdependently.

Heads of nations, CEOs, start-up founders, housewives, all handle multiple things routinely, using diverse and non-competing resources. Of course, we must see how much we can handle at a time. In the end, it also depends on our unique nature.

How Long Does It Take? And How Will One Know?

How long it takes for us to create a new pattern depends on how much actual work needs to be put in to develop that pattern well. Certain patterns might take no time at all to adopt, as those are only a matter of understanding and taking a decision. Certain other patterns that need a lot of work to repattern, might take much longer, even years.

The time that we take is a function of our level of knowledge and clarity, and our current level of skills. Our method and technique need to be right.

It is important to note that while a new neural network

gets created, the older ones are still there. If we slacken, our mind will switch back immediately to the older pattern because it has not gone anywhere. To truly change, we have to make the current pattern so strong and make the older one so weak through disuse that the latter stands no chance against the former one. It is then that a pattern is truly changed. This applies to our bodily, emotional and action patterns, too.

On reaching the inflection point, wherein we start seeing rapid results, everything will seem to start falling in place on its own.

Lastly, getting to a new destination might take time, but facing a new direction will only take a moment. Once we face the new direction, each new step takes us towards the new destination. That is how simple it is.

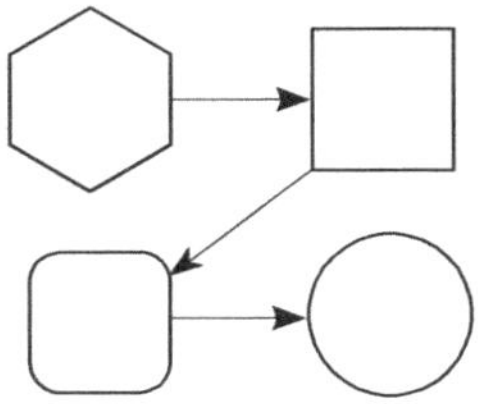

15

The E of PACE: Evolve Your Patterns

'What you do speaks so loudly that
I cannot hear what you say.'

—Ralph Waldo Emerson, essayist

Once conscious patterns become our default way of life, there is no limit to where and how we can apply our consciousness and patterns.

So far, we have focussed only on how to create the patterns of our bodies, minds, emotions, actions and environment. We have not touched upon any specific goals for which we could use these patterns. In this chapter, we will look at two such goals, related to our organizations and children.

But first, let us understand fractals, which are patterns within patterns.

Fractals

A fractal is a complex geometrical shape, with each part having the same statistical character as the whole. This means that when we zoom in on a fractal, smaller copies of the overall shape emerge. Each copy contains intricate details similar to the whole.

Fig. 15.1: Fractals

The preceding figure is a fractal. It is a triangle that has an infinite number of identical triangles within it.

Fractals can be found in nature, such as in the structure of a snowflake, etc. Here, however, I have used the term metaphorically to hint at anything that can be replicated almost endlessly. In this sense, McDonald's model of creating almost identical outlets around the world, using an excellent basic blueprint, has made the said company a fractal.

The power of fractals is unfathomable. They are never-ending. They are difficult to eliminate or destroy. Cut one branch of a tree and another one grows, similar to it. Destroy one cell in your body and another one appears.

Humans have learnt from fractals in nature. The internet is a fractal and so is Google—a never-ending and self-perpetuating information network. Multilevel marketing schemes are fractals. McDonald's and every other perpetuating franchise is a fractal too, with self-propagating branches and outlets.

Creating fractals is simple:

- Create one blueprint of value.
- Then find a way to multiply it. This means making multiple copies of the blueprint.

You can multiply a fractal by:

- Creating a network with a conscious centre that controls the growth of that network. In the McDonald's model, the company headquarters (or certain designated headquarters) creates and controls thousands of nearly identical McDonald's outlets around the world.
- Training the limbs themselves to propagate the chains. This creates self-perpetuating fractals, like email or WhatsApp forwards asking you to forward them further. The business networking company, BNI (Business Networking International), is one such organization. The company consist of zones in various cities around the world, which are designed to create more zones.

Covering fractals would need another book. Fractals are essentially patterns, and they place awesome power in our hands. This power can be seen all around us—in business, finance, volunteering, retailing, networking, you name it. In software, the open-source movement is a fractal of unending software developers who voluntarily develop and maintain software solutions that compete with mega-corporations.

Both patterns and fractals use the same basic technique. They create a small, simple and well-thought-out blueprint. Then they consciously repeat it.

Patterns and Organizations

Up until the 1990s, New York was one of the least safe cities in the world. Serious crimes, like murders and muggings, were commonplace. In 1994, the newly appointed Police Commissioner of New York, William Joseph Bratton, changed this pattern.[55]

Bratton applied James Q. Wilson and George Kelling's 'Broken Windows' theory. The theory says that crime emanates from broken windows—a metaphor used for disorder and incivility. It says that if you remove the underlying minor cases of disorder and incivility, then serious crimes would not occur.

Applying this theory, Bratton cracked down on New York. He started improving the rundown condition of New York's subway trains, train stations, turnstiles, etc. The police force went after small things that were amiss. For example, as many times as hooligans painted graffiti on trains, the police force got these trains repainted!

Bratton went after the root problems rather than going just after serious crimes. By the time he resigned in 1996, serious crime rates in New York had plummeted. The homicide rate in New York had dropped to half![56]

Organizations are disciplines of people and things. Therefore, patterns are applicable to organizations, too. We can either try to control our organizations or create little blueprints, like a clear vision, mission and values, systems, processes, resources,

[55]Bratton, W.J., and P. Knobler, *Turnaround: How America's Top Cop Reversed the Crime Epidemic*, Random House, 2009.
[56]Ibid.

automations, processes to add and grow talent, skills and capabilities, etc.

Such patterns run our organization's routines from day to day. Patterns also make our organizations flexible. To change a truly well-defined, laid-out and measured system is much easier than to disrupt chaos and find a way. In chaos, one doesn't even know what to change, unless one defines change as dumping everything and starting afresh each time!

The basic patterns of an organization must be carefully thought out and put in place, for they profoundly affect how an organization performs.

The armed forces, as an organization, understand and use the power of patterns. The patterns they build create a culture that outlasts even the organization. Look at military veterans anywhere and you will understand the truth behind this.

Patterns and Your Children

Imagine if your children were to start using the power of patterns consciously. If they could imbibe the right patterns at the right age, their lives would become so powerful. They would never be held back by their pasts. Instead, they would be free to act and simply be.

But also remember that your children are unique, just like you. Try not to just fit them into templates. Instead, allow and teach your children to be aware, conscious and also explore. Help them understand the power of conscious patterns. They will do the rest themselves.

Let children be close to nature as it is perhaps the greatest teacher.

Set good examples for your children. Be careful with your

own patterns around them. More than learning from your words, they tend to pick up from your actions, emotions and energies.

The Never-Ending Story

The only thing constant in life is change. Why should it be any different with patterns?

The beauty of our universe is in its inherent unpredictability. Besides, the universe is never still. It is ever-changing and evolving. But even our entropic universe has patterns that underlie its inherent unpredictability and make it more knowable.

But our patterns must be flexible and adaptable to deal with the inherent unpredictability of our world. Remember that patterns are our tools. Just as we change the way we use our resources when in water instead of land, we must change our patterns whenever required.

As time passes, many things change—our jobs, locations, situations in life, etc. Our capabilities, the technologies around us, the resources available, and even the social norms keep changing. Patterns are not a one-time thing; they are a way of life. Conscious patterns that keep us in the moment can even help us re-pattern ourselves in the next moment.

My only learning in life has been that there is no end to learning. Every answer is a fractal that leads to new questions and newer answers. Only certain fundamentals never seem to change. Seeking for and consciously creating patterns to seek success with self-mastery and fulfilment appears to be one such fundamental.

I think nature meant it to be so…

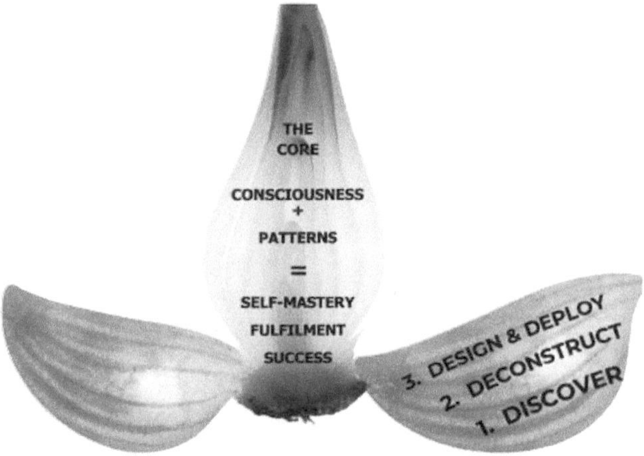

Layer IV: The Core of the Onion: Success with Self-Mastery and Fulfilment

'Thus self-fulfillment leaves more room for creativity than does self-actualization: in fulfilling oneself one creates oneself in that one creates both one's powers (by giving them determinate form) and one's developed states or activities. This development is shaped by one's aspirations, which help to mould one's implicit powers as well as the ends toward which they are directed.'

—Alan Gewirth, *Self-Fulfillment*

16

Success with Self-Mastery and Fulfilment

'All fixed set patterns are incapable of adaptability or pliability. The truth is outside of all fixed patterns.'

—Bruce Lee, martial artist and actor

You now know how to create and modify your patterns. And now you have reached the core of the onion of patterns—the secret to attaining success with self-mastery and fulfilment.

Here lies a surprising secret that might change how you think about success and failure. But before getting to that secret, let us revisit our friends Sam and Anita one last time.

A year ago, Sam and Anita had finally gathered the courage and taken the plunge into entrepreneurship. They had quit their jobs and started a custom software development firm.

Over the next year, they had hired a team and put in all the processes that they could to streamline their company. They also worked on their own business skills and started doing quite well.

One day, they found themselves in the midst of a crisis. They sat down with their business consultant.

'We just didn't see it coming,' said Sam. 'All was going well. Then suddenly our biggest client pulled out—they were helping us get 70 per cent of our total revenue!'

'How are you placed in terms of reserves?' their consultant asked.

'Barely any. We just upgraded our office,' Anita replied.

'But didn't we agree on this the last time we met? That we must not touch our reserves yet? And that we must urgently diversify our client base?"

'Yes,' Anita said and added, 'but the office needed an upgrade.'

Their consultant smiled. To him, it seemed like a repetition of similar conversations with clients in the past.

'I'm glad this has happened at this stage. We can start looking at how...'

'What?' Sam almost yelled. 'What do you mean you are glad?'

'Why not?' the consultant said calmly. 'We spoke about the golden rule of never putting all your eggs in one basket. We discussed that relying on a single client for most of your revenue is like committing hara-kiri. We also discussed that you must start creating a reserve for contingencies. Yet you did not act, as you believed that something like this would never happen to you.'

The consultant paused. 'Today, you can still salvage the situation by cutting corners. But imagine what could have happened. At the rate at which you are growing, your company will be four times its current size soon. Would you have been able to sustain the shock at that stage? In all likelihood, your company would have shut down!'

Sam and Anita looked shell-shocked.

The consultant softened his tone, 'You are looking at this as "failure". What if you look at this as an amazing message instead, one that is telling you what is wrong and what you must correct immediately?'

'Hmmm...' Anita said thoughtfully.

This is something that we must know. While we always aim at success, it is failure that teaches us the most in our lives. The study below will show you why this is so.

Patterns and Failures

'Failures persist despite remarkable individual ability.'

—Atul Gawande, *The Checklist Manifesto*

Let us understand why failures are also the route to lasting success.

In the 1970s, two philosophers Samuel Gorovitz and Alasdair MacIntyre published a short essay titled 'Towards a Theory of Medical Fallibility'.[57] They wanted to examine human fallibility in the medical context. They wanted to find out why people fail at things.

---

[57]Gorovitz, Samuel, and Alasdair MacIntyre, 'Towards a Theory of Medical Fallibility', Hastings Center Report, 5 December 1975.

Their findings were simple but profound. They found that leaving aside the inherent unpredictability in a given situation, people fail only due to two simple reasons:

(a) ignorance, which is not knowing how to do something; or
(b) ineptitude, which is failing to apply their knowledge correctly.

In the case of Sam and Anita, they knew what to do, but they failed to apply that knowledge.

Failure, like the good adviser it is, sent them a strong message, showing them the consequences of their mistakes.

This is why failure is so important. It does not soft talk. It tells us the truth bluntly through consequences. If we listen to it, it shows us our mistakes. It is on us to correct those.

Seen in this manner, our failures are the most important signposts along our path to success.

Virender Sehwag, the brilliant batsman of the Indian cricket team of the 1990s and 2000s, scored the highest number of runs ever in an innings in cricket. He, however, also had the highest number of ducks (zeros) to his credit. Without those ducks, he could have never become the highest scorer.

Reggie Jackson, the legendary American baseball player, scored 1,551 runs during his career, which is among the highest in baseball history. But he also struck out 2,597 times, which was a record at the time of his retirement. Successful people court defeat as the route to success.

Martial artist Bruce Lee put it beautifully, 'What is defeat? Nothing but education; nothing but the first step to something better.'

We blame our failures only so that we can give up without accepting responsibility.

In fact, it is a myth that success evolves in a straight line. In reality, success means walking, stumbling, learning and getting up to continue walking. Fluke successes can make us forget the greatest lessons in life. Failures help us root out our ignorance and ineptitudes. Failures are never wrong; we are.

Atul Gawande writes in *The Checklist Manifesto*: 'We don't look for patterns of our recurrent mistakes or devise and refine potential solutions for them.'[58] The crux of this is that failures follow patterns, too. Once we are able to identify patterns in our failures, we will know which patterns need to be changed.

Patterns Lead to Success along with Self-Mastery and Fulfilment

Conscious patterns are a way of life. With our patterns, we create the frame—the outlines—of the jigsaw puzzle that is our life. With the frame in place, we keep fitting in new pieces as they come to us.

And this leads us to:

- **Self-mastery:** It helps us gain mastery over ourselves and our environment.
- **Success and fulfilment:** We experience happiness, success and fulfilment as we move towards, arrive at, and move beyond our goals. If the moments leading to

---

[58]Gawande, Atul, *Checklist Manifesto: How to Get Things Right*, Penguin Random House India, 2009, p. 185.

> a destination are not fulfilling, is that destination even of value? Further, patterns, when used correctly, also help us set our goal compass towards self-actualization (the top of Maslow's hierarchy of needs), rather than towards the lower needs (physiological needs, safety, love and belonging, and esteem).

To understand this, consider the following example. You bought your car to travel to places. But to be able to use that car to go anywhere, you must keep it in a good condition, keep it safe, and so on. But can any of these things, for example just keeping a car safe, serve the purpose of the car?

Similarly, is your purpose in life to be merely physiologically sound, safe, loved and respected, without ever doing anything of value? In fact, these two things, the means and the end, are built to support one another.

After all, as Bruce Lee said, 'A goal is not always meant to be reached, it often serves simply as something to aim at.'

Play to win without getting too attached to the results. Our universe is probabilistic. So, focus on building patterns consciously and you will see the results eventually.

Epilogue

'A problem well-stated is half-solved.'

—Charles Kettering, American inventor and engineer

Finding the right word to express something is like asking the right question. The answer follows. My search for patterns was about finding the right word. I already knew that habits matter. Yet, habits do not provide a complete answer to the human conundrum; they only scratch the surface when it comes to explaining who we are. Habits are effects, and to change them, one must find and change the causes.

Stumbling upon the immensity of this simple word 'patterns' sounded like the clashing of cymbals in my head. It was like a fog lifting from around me. In an instant, so many things became crystal clear. Habits fell into place. Unconscious, subconscious and conscious actions, thoughts, emotions and energy began to make sense.

Amazingly, even the eightfold path or eight limbs of yoga, as outlined by the Sage Patanjali in the Yoga Sutras, to reach the same goal of self-realization—something that had always mystified me—also began to make absolute sense.

Patterns are a fundamental construct of nature. We have

always been using this construct to make sense of ourselves and our world. We have even given names to common patterns, like the laws of mathematics, sciences, arts, our languages and our habits.

Yet, somewhere, this categorization overwrites and obscures the simplicity of the core. Simply put, that core is the presence of patterns, above which is the conscious awareness. To set something right, we just need to correct the underlying patterns. And to do that correctly, we need conscious awareness. Such patterns then become conscious patterns. Otherwise, they are unconscious, subconscious or barely understood.

Overall, our patterns support our conscious self. They help us create beauty and complexity from simplicity. That is all there is to it.

But why this obsession with patterns, you may ask? In patterns, I see a solution to the distortions created in our world.

As we saw earlier, Samuel Gorovitz and Alasdair MacIntyre found the causes of most medical failures to be ignorance and ineptitude. To me, this appears to apply to the entire human race and to the entire human context. As a race, we have remained mostly unaware of the fundamental nature of the world around us. In spite of our intense curiosity, we have remained blind to much that should have been obvious. We have relied too much on our limited intellect and limited ourselves to 'our knowledge'.

We have, therefore, conducted our worldly affairs like a blind person with a sword. The results have been disastrous. The distortions that we have caused to our world, to our climate and to our own lifestyles sometimes seem too huge to repair, but there is always hope.

In 1950, Thomas A. Harris wrote in his book *I'm OK, You're OK*: 'The problems of the world—and they are chronicled daily in headlines of violence and despair—essentially are the problems of individuals. If individuals can change, the course of this world can change. This is a hope worth sustaining.'[59]

In patterns, there might be the answer to much of the distortions that we observe around us.

To get to the right results, in addition to the right intentions, we also need to possess the right knowledge and methods. This means understanding and correcting things at the level of the basic patterns. The end alone does not matter. The means, too, must be correct.

Therefore, perhaps it is in understanding and straightening our fundamental patterns where our answers can be found. We have created the distortions that exist in our world with our tiny actions. With tiny patterns, we can correct them too. No huge pushes and shoves are needed. All we need are the slightest of repeated nudges, in the right places, using the right techniques.

Examples of Common Patterns

It is neither possible nor is it the aim of this book to be an encyclopaedia of good patterns. At the end of the book, some useful everyday patterns have been listed. This is just to give you an idea of what kinds of patterns you might need for success along with self-mastery and fulfilment.

---

[59]Harris, Thomas Anthony, *I'm OK - You're OK,* Jonathan Cape Ltd, 1967, p. xvii.

Check whether some of these patterns fit your needs. You can modify them to suit yourself. Use the ones that serve you in some way. Patterns are there not to enslave you but to set you free.

Appendices[60]

[60]It is not possible to cover all patterns in the appendices. These are micro-samples. Adopt and adapt only those that suit you.

Section 1

Sample Patterns

Shaping Your Environment

If there is anything we ignore more than our own selves, it is our environment. How we manage what is external to ourselves affects us massively.

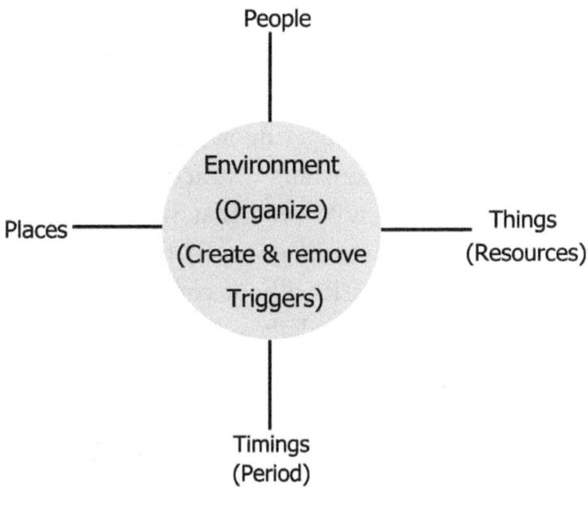

Fig. i: What to shape in your environment and how

Here are a few sample patterns.

- Organize your environment:
  - As mentioned earlier, your first step should be to deconstruct, simplify and organize your surroundings and even your data bank(s). Recognize that your capabilities have limited channel capacities. Group things together into meaningful clusters. Fix a place for all routine things. For example, you can place your keys in a specific spot in your home or a particular pocket when you are leaving home.
  - Throw away all that is meaningless. You can read *The Life-Changing Magic of Tidying Up* by Marie Kondo. Organize your electronic data, back it up in easily retrievable folders. Delete files that are rarely used or create a dump where you can put the things you are not using. Clear that dump periodically.
  - Organize all your tasks—now and for the future—in one place, rather than having these coming at you from everywhere. The aim should be not to have any tasks lingering at the back of your mind, causing you constant distraction and stress. Your brain should hold only that which it can manage with ease. This will give you the time to focus on your current task without constant distraction.
  - Some people use daily schedulers to list the day's important tasks. There is a caution to scheduling. If you schedule something, do it!
- Make your environment enabling enough by inserting suitable triggers. Use coasters, mats, charts, boards, passwords, songs and other things to facilitate the

patterns you want in your life.

- Focus on the people in your life. They are amongst the most significant causes behind why your life is the way it is.

Section 2

Your Body

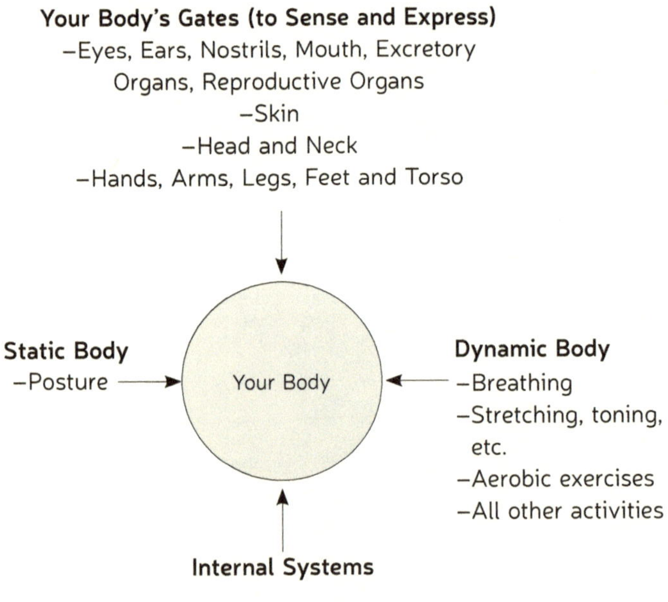

Fig. ii: An overview of your body

Yoga is widely regarded as an effective means to enhance physical well-being. Other sciences and disciplines that focus on physical well-being, improving posture, movement efficiency and overall body coordination include disciplines like Pilates, t'ai chi, martial arts, etc.

Here are a few body patterns for you to consider:

- **Posture:** Posture refers to the position and alignment of the body while sitting, standing, lying, moving, etc. Our posture patterns affect us in many ways.
  - Lying down: One-third to one-sixth of our existence is spent lying down. Journals, such as *Sleep Medicine* and *Journal of Clinical Sleep Medicine,* often publish research studies related to sleep postures and their effects on sleep quality, energy levels and overall health. I have found that my sleeping posture affects even my dreams. Sleeping on your side is often recommended by healthcare professionals and perhaps comes naturally to most people. When we are lying down correctly, we feel totally relaxed and rested. You can also seek expert advice.
  - Sitting and standing: The consequences of sitting and standing in incorrect postures for hours at a stretch each day far outstrip the effects of any daily 30-minute exercise routine. Adopt healthy postures. Sit with your spine erect, ensure that your reading material is a little below eye level. Many people these days have started sitting on the floor even in their office premises. I do that, too. Once again, I would suggest you to seek expert advice.
  - Walking and running: Walking barefoot on grass is excellent. You can follow this at home at least. Bad shoes can impact your heels, ankles, legs, knees,

hips, spine and neck. When it comes to wearing shoes, the ones with flat soles should be preferred. Discard shoes with worn-out soles. I am bow-legged. My shoe soles wear out on the outer sides. So, I stick flat-headed nails in my shoe soles on the outer sides to prevent uneven wear and tear.

- **Stretching and toning exercises:** Our physical body is a mass of muscles, ligaments, bones, organs, etc. Keeping them fit forms the foundation for a good life and for all-round success. Stretching and toning exercises can make a huge difference. A few deep stretches daily can keep your body supple and flexible.
- **Aerobic exercises:** Aerobic exercises help build stamina. A daily walk or run and a few daily sit-ups and push-ups can make you much fitter and alter your physique. However, pick up patterns that suit you best. You can walk, run, use the stairs, cycle, swim, dance, go to the gym, play a sport, do martial arts, and so on. You can even use a combination and move from one exercise to another. Some people enjoy exercising in groups. Some like walking a dog. Others like walking with friends. Do whatever works best for you. Also, whatever routine you decide to follow, make it convenient for yourself. For example, if you start going to the gym, find a gym on your route to work, place a gym bag in your car, create a gym at home, and so on.
- **Body weight:** Weight gain in your body is the difference between how much you take in and how much your body is able to burn or consume. Of these two, find out what is out of balance. If it is a medical condition,

see a doctor. And, like everything else, thinking that you are fit also keeps you fit!

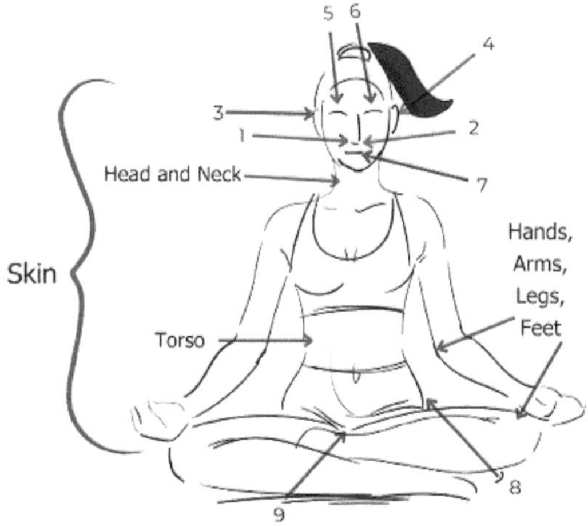

Fig. iii: Your body. The numbers 1 to 9 indicate the entry and exit points of your body

- **Sensory organs:** In yoga, all entry and exit points of the body are considered extremely important. Today, almost everyone wears glasses and suffers from some eye problem or the other. Many are deaf or close to it, and do not even know about it.
  - Eyes:
    - Have you noticed the remarkable improvement in your reading ability when you read in the sunlight? Working in natural light is perhaps the best pattern to adopt. Shape your environment such that you can facilitate this pattern.
    - The rising sun is excellent for our eyes. Looking towards the early morning sun, without staring

directly at it, can help you maintain perfect vision.
    - Frequent resting, palming and splashing your closed eyes with water are good exercises. Palming involves rubbing your palms together and covering your eyes with your palms. It is very relaxing. You can palm your eyes during breaks and wash them whenever you wash your hands.
    - Use the 20–20–20 technique when reading or writing for longer periods. Every 20 minutes, look at something 20 feet away for 20 seconds.
    - The School for Perfect Eyesight, a unit of Sri Aurobindo Ashram in Puducherry, India, recommends many practices for eyesight correction. You may find videos related to this on YouTube.[61]
    - Find fun ways of improving your eyesight. I sit in my sunlit balcony every morning, read my favourite books, keep my juggling balls on my table, and keep an eye patch handy for resting and exercising each eye.
  - Ears:
    - Protect your ears from loud music and noise. Avoid excessive use of headphones.
    - Practise good ear hygiene. But be cautious of not damaging your ears.
    - The decline in your hearing abilities may result

[61]'School for Perfect Eyesight Eye Routines Part 1 | Sri Aurobindo Ashram | Finding of RS & MS Agarwal', YouTube, https://tinyurl.com/y3p5mpya. Accessed on 24 April 2024.

in a loss of social connections, potentially leading to numerous challenges. Monitor your hearing health and, if required, consult a healthcare professional.

- Mouth: Refer to the next section on food.
- Nose:
  - The book *Science of Breath* states, 'The science of pranayama is thus intimately connected with the autonomic nervous system and brings its functions under conscious control through the functioning of the lungs.'[62] This is neither mysticism nor an exaggeration. Breathing is the only bodily function that is both voluntary and involuntary. It is the link to our involuntary systems. To understand this, just calm your breathing. You will notice that it also immediately calms your heart rate, perspiration, emotions and mind. This connection extends to all involuntary or autonomic systems.
  - Additionally, '...a change in the breathing pattern can also alter the emotional state as well as effect physiological changes in the body.'[63] To quote the same book, 'It is for this reason that control of the breath constitutes an obvious starting point toward the attainment of control over the functioning of the autonomous nervous system.'[64]

[62]Rama, Swami, Allan Hymes and Rudolph Ballentine, *Science of Breath*, Pennsylvania, The Himalayan Institute Press, 1998, p. 76.
[63]Ibid. 36.
[64]Ibid. 76.

Correcting your basic body geometry and patterns as you go about your day is more than half the battle won. You can dovetail most of this into your daily routines. You can also exercise for a few minutes or an hour daily, or a few times a week.

Section 3

You Are What You Eat

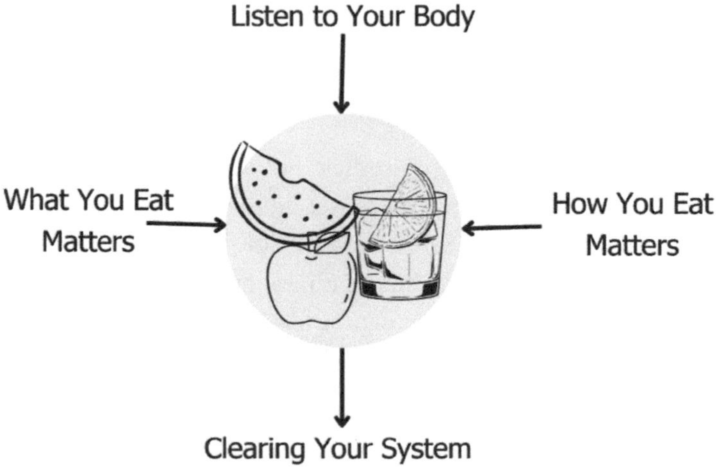

Fig. iv: Tips related to eating well

Every culture understands the importance of food:

'Don't dig your grave with your own knife and fork.'

—An English proverb

'Eat breakfast like a king, lunch like a prince and dinner like a beggar.'

—An Arab proverb

'Jaisa ann, vaisa mann (You are what you eat).'

—A Hindi proverb

Traditional solutions to most problems lay in consuming or avoiding the consumption of something. Our food and breathing provide almost all the essential elements that comprise our bodies, minds, emotions and energies. A quick calculation will show that if we have three regular meals each day, it will equal to around 87,600 meals over an 80-year lifetime, excluding snacking.

There are countless studies on food but the motives behind many are suspect because, unfortunately, it is also the route to our pockets. Selective statistics can make you believe anything. The effects of this madness are extreme.

Please conduct your own study on food or check with trusted experts. As for me, I follow these three simple food rules, which work well for me:

- I listen to my body, not just my stomach. The human body is an incredible machine that usually knows what is best for it. Whenever one feels an urge to eat something, one's body usually needs it. Whenever one's body doesn't need something, it is quick to throw it out. So, I do not let my stomach or external triggers override my basic intelligence. Therefore, whenever I eat only to satisfy my taste buds or only for an experience (which is fine too, but as an exception), my body and mind always stop me from overeating.

- Supermarkets are economically driven to almost always use the cheapest food alternatives that are not legally banned. Their survival depends not on making one healthier but on remaining competitive. So, I go for fresh, natural foods that are not bio-engineered. For packaged foods, I read the labels very carefully.
- All cultures have adapted to local foods. I prefer locally grown food products as my body is probably best adapted to those. However, this is difficult to always follow in today's world.
- I find traditional food options reliable, as they are backed by centuries of empirical proof. There are hundreds of simple, convenient, healthy, tasty and non-controversial food options. While reading up research articles on food, I make sure to check for proper sources.

- I feel that how I eat matters a lot—having a good breakfast, light lunch and lighter dinner, along with a reasonable amount of water. I chew my food well and enjoy my food. I do not rush through it. I also rest my digestive system periodically by simply eating fruits or fasting.
- It is important to clear our system of waste and toxins every day. Holding these inside our body loads our system with toxins and also kills our energy. I start my day with one or two glasses of room temperature water. It gives me much-needed hydration and also clears my system.

Section 4

Your Mind and Thoughts

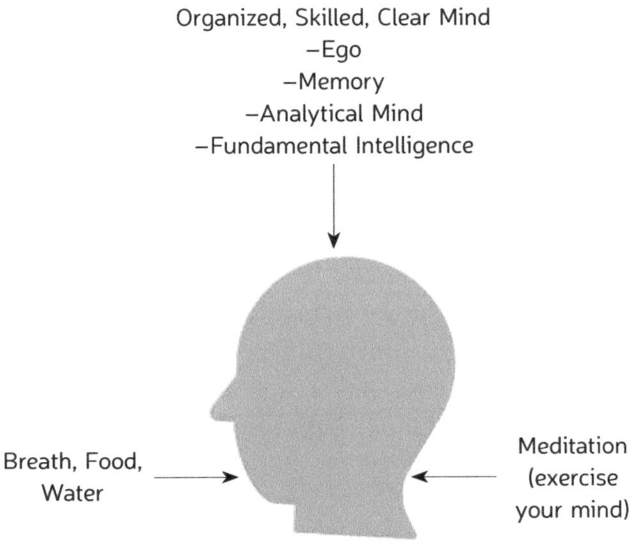

Fig. v: Mind and related patterns

The yogic system classifies the mind into four fundamental parts—intellect, identity, memory and pure intelligence.

The ideal mind should be aware, organized and reflective.

The mind should be in control. It should be able to reflect on the past, imagine the future while living in the present. Our powerful underlying intelligence should be free and available to guide us. Patterns that can bring our mind to such a state are as follows:

- **Decluttered and clear mind**
  - A cluttered mind, resulting from a chaotic environment, leads to confusion and flits incessantly from one thing to another. All your senses are under assault. Hence, you should organize your environment.
  - Rid your mind of the junk it collects. Begin to learn how to let go. The most successful people are ones who are in control of their minds. They are aware of everything but engage with limited quantity of information at a time. The very little that they choose to focus upon is far more effective than the thousand things that they decide to let go. Try it. It will amaze you.
  - A good memory is a huge asset. This, too, is the result of a clutter-free and well-organized mind. Paying attention, association with existing memories and repetition are proven techniques to improve memory. Here are a few great memory patterns:
    - Mentally reviewing your entire day before going to bed makes your memory razor sharp.
    - Journaling is an amazing aid to memory and clarity. You can keep a diary by your bedside to remind you to journal every day.
    - For students, a concept understood once and

revisited regularly becomes far easier to retain than spending hours in one go on that concept.

        - Charts, pictures, a vision board and other visual or sensory triggers make it far easier to grasp and recall concepts. A friend lined his room walls with military campaigns. In no time, he knew them better than the back of his hand.

    - Start listening to your fundamental intelligence more than to the twin monkeys, namely ego and your intellect, as both can lead you astray.

- **Breathing, food and water**
    - Breathing is fundamental to meditation. It fuels our brain, mind, emotions and actions. Make steady and rhythmic breathing your default pattern. Food and water, too, form the basics of a healthy and powerful mind. The book *Gut and Psychology Syndrome* by Dr Natasha Campbell-McBride describes the gut–mind relationship. It describes how blood carries nutrients from food first to the brain. It explores the idea that poor gut health can influence the functioning of the brain and potentially contribute to conditions like autism and ADHD.
- **Meditation**
    - Meditation involves exercise of the mind that leads to awareness, mental clarity, agility and control over the mind. Meditation, like any muscle, grows through repeated practice, so do not expect results from the first day itself. Find a good meditation practitioner to understand it better. Regular meditation, as a pattern, rather than infrequent meditation, is much more effective. Place triggers to remind yourself to

meditate on a daily basis. You can also anchor your meditation practice to a time slot that suits you.

- Setting aside some quiet time to sit with yourself without an agenda is a needed exercise for your brain. This allows your mind to reflect and explore. Keep a paper and pencil handy to list the thoughts that strike you. This will help you find clarity.[65]
- Observe your thoughts. The 12,000–60,000 thoughts that you have daily follow a handful of patterns. Blamers blame, escapers look for escape, and joyful people find joy in everything. Remember to observe the patterns of your thoughts. That is the first step to changing them.

---

[65]J., Canfield, Mark Victor Hansen and L. Hewitt, *The Power of Focus: How to Hit Your Business, Personal, and Financial Targets with Confidence and Certainty*, Health Communications, 2011.

Section 5

Emotions

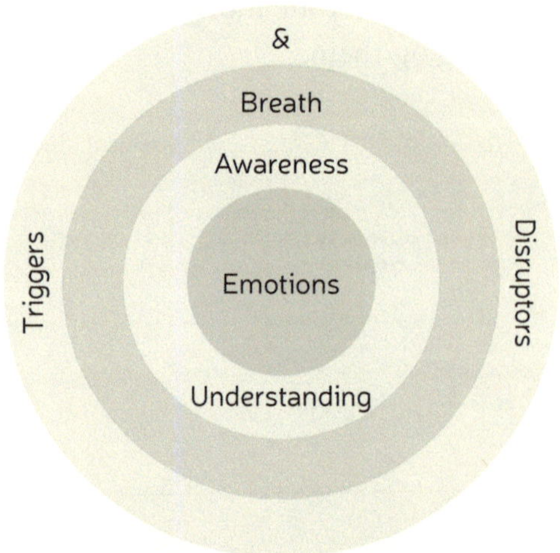

Fig. vi: An overview of how to master your emotions

Our emotions are too powerful to be left without being understood and controlled. If we don't manage our emotions, they'll end up controlling us.

The aim is not to be emotionless but to establish a control over emotions:

- Step one is to understand and review your emotions. Ask yourself: 'What are my emotions and where do they come from?' After any spontaneous emotional outburst or failure to control it, ask what caused it. Was there an external trigger or/and a deeper internal reason? Can you do a root analysis? Can you dig into your past? Could you have avoided it? What can you do to change that pattern in the future? Can you remove the triggers that set off such emotions? Can you use disruptors? Can you take deep breaths, count from 1 to 5, or count backwards to overcome a blocker?
- Similarly, for emotions like happiness, look for reasons yourself. Surround yourself with triggers that lead to desirable emotions. When you see a baby, you cannot help smiling. When a dog wags its tail, you feel happy. When you talk to a friend, you are empathetic. When you experience the beauty of nature, you feel peaceful and grateful.
- Alter your respiratory rhythm. Make it regular and even, not irregular and jagged. Swami Rama says, 'Because emotions are clearly related to the breath, by altering our respiratory rhythm, we should be able to shift emotional gears.'[66]

---

[66]Rama, Swami, Allan Hymes and Rudolph Ballentine, *Science of Breath, Pennsylvania*, Himalayan Institute Press Honesdale, 1998, p. 17.

Section 6

Actions

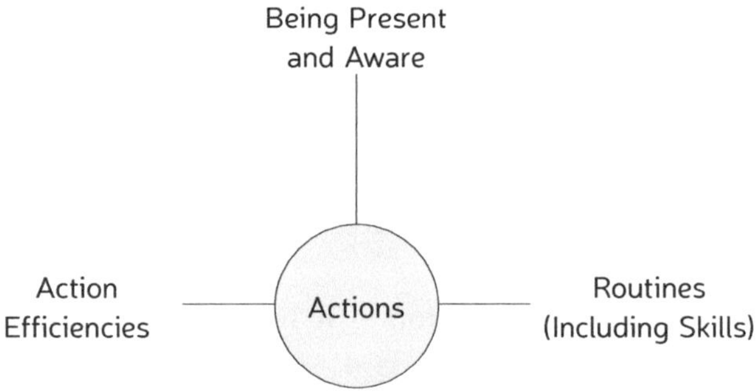

Fig. vii: An overview of your actions and related issues

Energy expresses itself through change. Ultimately, whatever you are and whatever you aspire to is revealed through your actions alone. Therefore, even the most complex of all your pursuits can be traced back to the simplest of actions, which can be yours or that of the world.

You cannot always control the world around you. But you can certainly control your own actions, directly or via their root causes.

Here are a few simple patterns you can consider:

- **Being present and aware:** Consciously lingering in the moment, away from past and future, is perhaps the most fundamental letting-go pattern. It is at the core of being curious, interested and alive.
- **Routines**
  - **Daily**
    - **The early morning ritual:** Early morning is the time when one can be the most productive. It is also perhaps most in line with our basic biorhythms. Many successful people start their work day around 3.00 a.m. or 3.30 a.m. Hindu tradition calls this time the Brahma Mudra or the 'time of creation'. During this period, schedule things that you really enjoy doing. These can be things for which you are not able to find time. It is a good time to take a walk, do deep breathing exercises and watch the predawn sky.
    - **Meal times:** These hours should be spent with the family; it would help you rejuvenate your body, mind, emotions and energy.
    - **At night:** Use this time to review and journal your day. Finish the day with pleasant thoughts before your head hits the pillow. Walking through the day gone by, step by step, before drifting off is also brilliant for planning the next day and for retaining the memory of the present one.
  - **Days of the week:** Earmarking days for certain tasks is great for batching and organizing. You can schedule meetings in and outside office on particular

days. Saturdays can be for planning the next week. You can reserve Mondays to meet, review and hit the ground running.

- **Skills:** All your higher-level pursuits can be broken down into skills that you can work on developing. For example, the management aspect of an event can be broken down into planning, delegating, communicating, etc. Deconstruct these skills down to their basic patterns and work upon those patterns.
- **Action efficiencies**
    - **Techniques:** The right techniques for doing recurring tasks, like speed reading, using all fingers to type, etc., can be powerful.
    - **Focus/concentration:** Build a pattern of concentrating on what is happening in the moment. Do this especially when listening or talking to someone, observing something or doing some task. Over time, this will become a pattern.
    - **An executive assistant:** Executive assistants help schedule meetings, check emails and social media accounts, make travel arrangements, do targeted research and a thousand other things. You can start with a morning meeting with your executive assistant to delegate everything possible, narrowing down your work.
    - **Networking and meetings:** Research about the people you are scheduled to meet. Using an application for recording meetings is an excellent tool for reference and recall (if allowed). Adding 'commitments made to people' to your to-do list can also help.

Section 7

Money and Financial Management

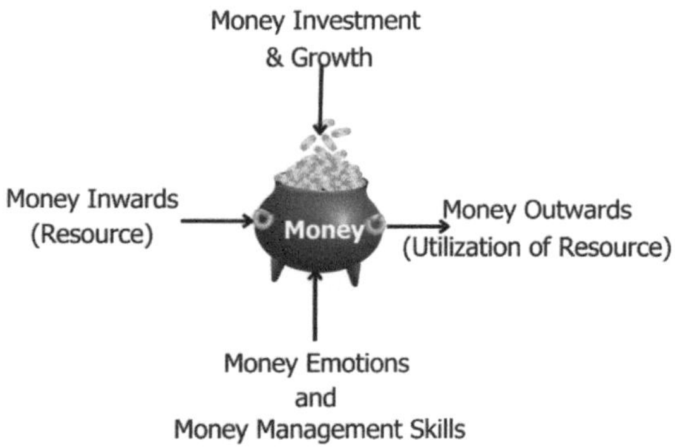

Fig. viii: The fundamentals of money management

We must grasp five fundamentals about money before we look at our money patterns:

- Money is a universally accepted currency that is used for transaction of goods and services. It is a resource that pervades every aspect of our social existence.
- Money represents latent energy through which we gather and release or block the energies of people and

other resources around us. We can pay workers and release their energies to get something done, or we can pay someone to block something from happening. Therefore, money is a very powerful resource.

- Our attitude and feelings towards money are shaped by our own root attitudes and feelings. If we are insecure, we use money to feel secure. If we feel less loved, we use money to try and buy love, and so on. If we feel a lack of worth, we seek self-worth through money. Money, therefore, becomes a universal channel to source the things we seek. It is not surprising, therefore, that money becomes a goal in itself. It begins to generate intense greed and fear in us.
- Good money management is first about correctly understanding and controlling our emotions related to money, like greed, fear, arrogance, shame, etc. Simply going after money, without analysing what you truly seek, will only make you feel more confused.
- Financial management skills—techniques to acquire, hold, invest and spend money—are important. To manage money well, you need these skills too. Poor money skills can make people incapable of holding or growing the money they have.

With these fundamentals in place, you can analyse your money management environment, thoughts, actions, emotions and energy. You will find patterns there. Also work on finding those that cause greed, fear of a lack of money, financial difficulties, etc. It is these patterns you must observe and set right. Some examples of such common patterns are listed below:

- **Find and root out unreasonable emotions about money:** My own emotions about money, or lack of it, resulted in not taking care of money till I realized that it, like any other resource, needs care too. I discovered a pattern of impulsiveness in the way I used to spend. This was checked the moment I understood that money decisions also need knowledge and skills, and I began to acquire them.
- **Learn money management:** If you are a businessperson, learn financial management for your business. Mike Michalowicz in his book *Profit First* teaches money discipline. He advises people to prioritize taking profits first and to restrict expenses to what is left. He advises regular investments for growth and opening separate accounts for different income and expense heads. Such rhythms are very effective in managing finances.
- **Inward flow of money:**
    - Money comes not from job or business; it comes from providing value. Create channels that keep money flowing inwards. The size of the trickle does not matter. Remember the power of compounding.
    - Give money, just as you give other things of value. Give now. You cannot be a miser today and turn into a giver in some imagined future. Do it even if you have to start small.
- **Money growth:**
    - Make investing a pattern. Create channels to invest. Investment allows someone else to put your money to use. It, therefore, multiplies your money. Remember that idle money depreciates and

is a wasted resource. Learn about investing from a trusted financial advisor.

- **Outward flow of money:**
    - Remove forgotten wastages that keep draining out money. This is not inclusive of channels that you consciously created to utilize money.
    - The greater the amount of money lying around, the more blocked energy it represents! I have a strategically placed piggy bank near my desk, in which I place the coins I find lying around the house. The piggy bank frequently funds surprise occasions!

Section 8

Your Work or Business

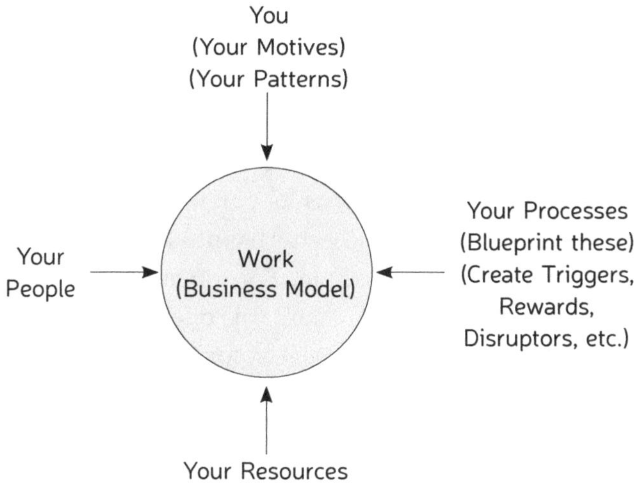

Fig. ix: Key patterns related to work or business

We create boundaries between our personal and professional lives. However, the patterns of our bodies, minds, emotions and actions affect the former and the latter equally.

Here are a few patterns that you can apply in your professional and personal life:

- Ideally, you must do work that gives you a sense of fulfilment. Clearly define the outcomes that you seek from your work. Clarity brings excitement. Visualize your work goals with the same clarity with which you visualize your personal goals. If you are not able to do that, then you need to reassess your work and your motives for doing that work.
- Whatever work you do is 99 per cent patterns. List your work-related successes and failures. Then analyse the patterns underlying them. In short, identify the patterns in your work environment and within yourself.
- Blueprint your work or business. Analyse and make a flowchart for all your key work systems and processes. Extract basic patterns and find root causes. Find correct techniques to drive those patterns and then create the right patterns as per your and your team's strengths. Turn these patterns into blueprints for easy reference and replication. For a business, these could be in the form of standard operating procedures (SOPs), checklists, templates, forms, samples, training videos, etc.
- Rewards, rather than words, drive actions. Create clear and positive rewards. If possible, create immediate rewards too. Immediate rewards best convey whatever you wish to convey.
- At work, managing people or teams is all about harnessing their aspirations to create whatever you want to create. If you can gather the right teams, whose aspirations match your aspirations, then they will help you attain your professional goals. If there

is a mismatch, then re-examine your work aspirations and those of your teams.

- Planning, organizing and decluttering are very important at work.

Section 9

Relationships

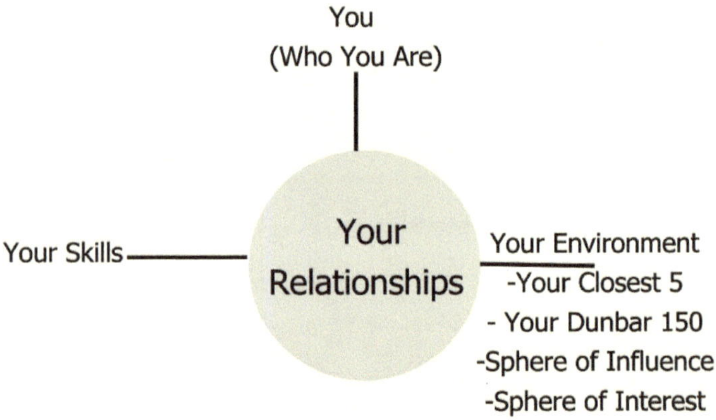

Fig. x: Factors that most affect your relationships

These days, terms like social media relationships, customer relationships, etc., tend to be greatly confusing in the context of our personal relationships. They are processes, not relationships, as the latter involves thinking about 'us'. Most relationship problems, therefore, are a result of our disproportionate preoccupation with our own selves.

Like everything, relationships too tend to follow patterns. Here are some basic patterns for healthy relationships:

- The ideal ego state in which good relationships flourish is, 'I'm okay, you're okay.' Relationships may even flourish in complementary ego states, wherein one person is authoritarian and the other is submissive. But such relationships cannot really be called healthy. Therefore, developing an ego state in which one holds high self-worth for oneself as well as others is the one ideal for great relationships.
- Healthy reciprocal relationships also mean dealing with others as you yourself would wish to be dealt with.
- The key patterns that support good relationships are genuineness, understanding, sharing (giving and accepting) with grace, and reliability. These patterns act like muscles too, as they grow through repetition or regular exercise. Create triggers and disruptors as and when needed.

Section 10

Hobbies, Passions, Leisure

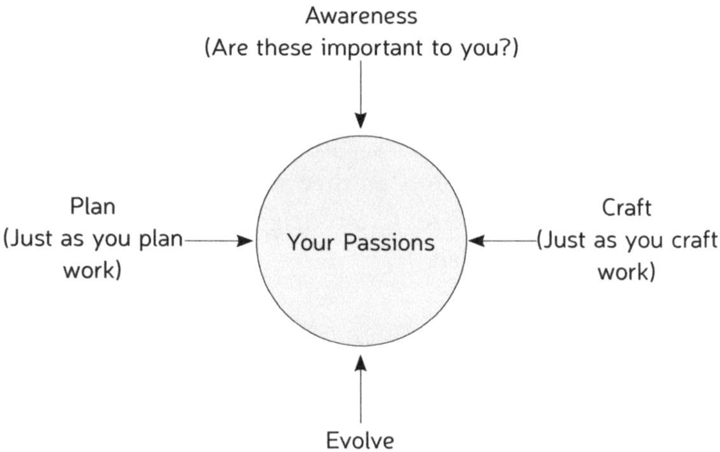

Fig. xi: How to nurture your passions

Passions and hobbies are means of self-expression, which is why they make us feel so good.

These are some of the patterns that you can consider for passions:

- Make your passions and hobbies a part of your life now, not later. Plan for your passions as you plan for the rest of your goals. Set aside time and resources for them. Place triggers to draw yourself towards your passions.
- The right technique is as important for your passion as it is for your work. If learning that demands money or time, invest in it. It will prove to be a priceless bargain.
- Try out new methods and techniques. First, learn what exists, then go beyond it. Bruce Lee first learnt kung fu. Then he went beyond and created his own martial arts form, *jeet kune do* (the way of the intercepting fist). He said, 'Absorb what is useful. Discard what is not. Add what is uniquely your own.'

Acknowledgements

All of us are meant to follow our own footsteps in life. My parents allowed my brother and me to do that, and supported us with their love and advice. To them, I owe everything. They are my anchors.

The English writer William Penn said, 'In marriage, do thou be wise: prefer the person before money, virtue before beauty, the mind before the body; then thou hast a wife, a friend, a companion, a second self.' My wife Archana is my friend, my companion and my second self. She is my mirror. She and my wonderful children, Abhinav and Shreya, saw value in the ideas that underlie this book. That is my greatest validation.

Abhinav tried throwing all the preachy words out of the book. Shreya drew the sketches. Arun, my brother, further refined the book. My parents-in-law supported me with their unshakeable faith. I lost my father-in-law recently. My mother-in-law continues to be an anchor.

My best friend, Biggles the Beagle, our dog, pretends to not listen and ignores us, but is always around when most needed.

Thank you, Paritosh Pathak, Rahul Jain and Rajiv Talreja—great coaches, friends and human beings; your advice is always selfless.

Ramana Metlapalli, my friend, meeting you was serendipity. You testing the concepts in the book, your exhaustive feedback and notes were invaluable in shaping this book.

All my friends helped in various ways. Vijay Pruthi, Kapil Arora, Vikas Bagga and R.K. Singh reposed their faith in me. Tabassum, Mukta Mani and Kanav Gupta acted as great connectors. Amit Chawla and Poonam Bhandari gave sound advice. Amit Mittal, Ashootosh Kant and many others ordered copies even before this book was published. What more could an author wish for.

Thank you to the attendees at my patterns workshops, all of whom shared invaluable experiences and feedback.

I have stood on the shoulders of giants to look farther. I have relied on their work to reach the conclusions arrived at in this book. Thank you all.

I thank my publisher, Rupa Publications, especially the commissioning editor Saswati Bora and copy editor Sakschi Verma, who painstakingly went through every single word in the book.

I would also like to thank my executive assistant, Sweety Kumari. Without her constant support, the book would never have been published.

I also beg forgiveness of all those who have been with me over the years, who have helped shape this book and whose names I have failed to mention. Thank you!

Most of all, thank you, dear reader. You compelled me to dig deeper. In trying to explain conscious patterns to you, I have grown. You are my leading light.

Your stories and opinions matter. They act as proof and raise questions that need answers. I invite you to play with the concepts in this book, and to share your stories, opinions and questions via https://sunilprem.com/conscious-human-patterns/

I eagerly look forward to them.